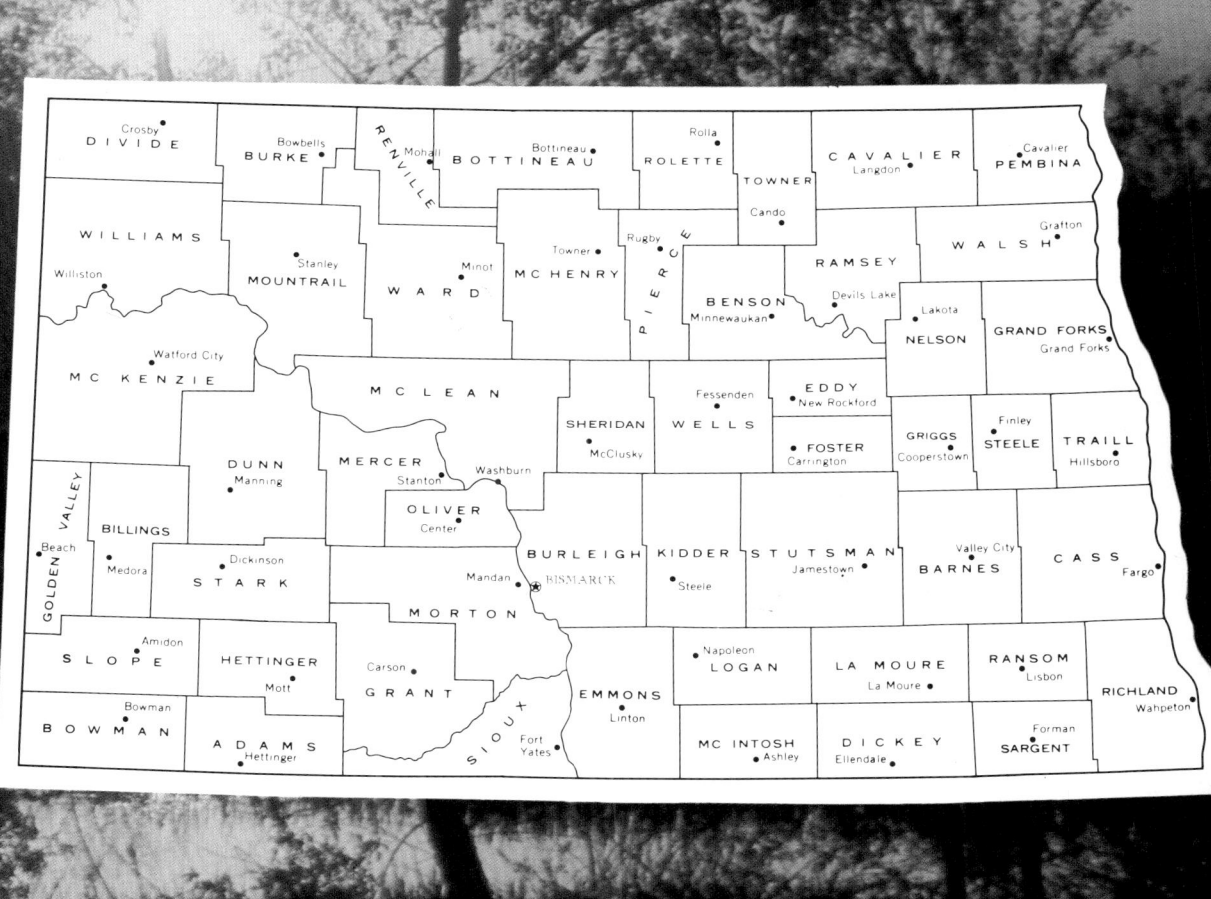

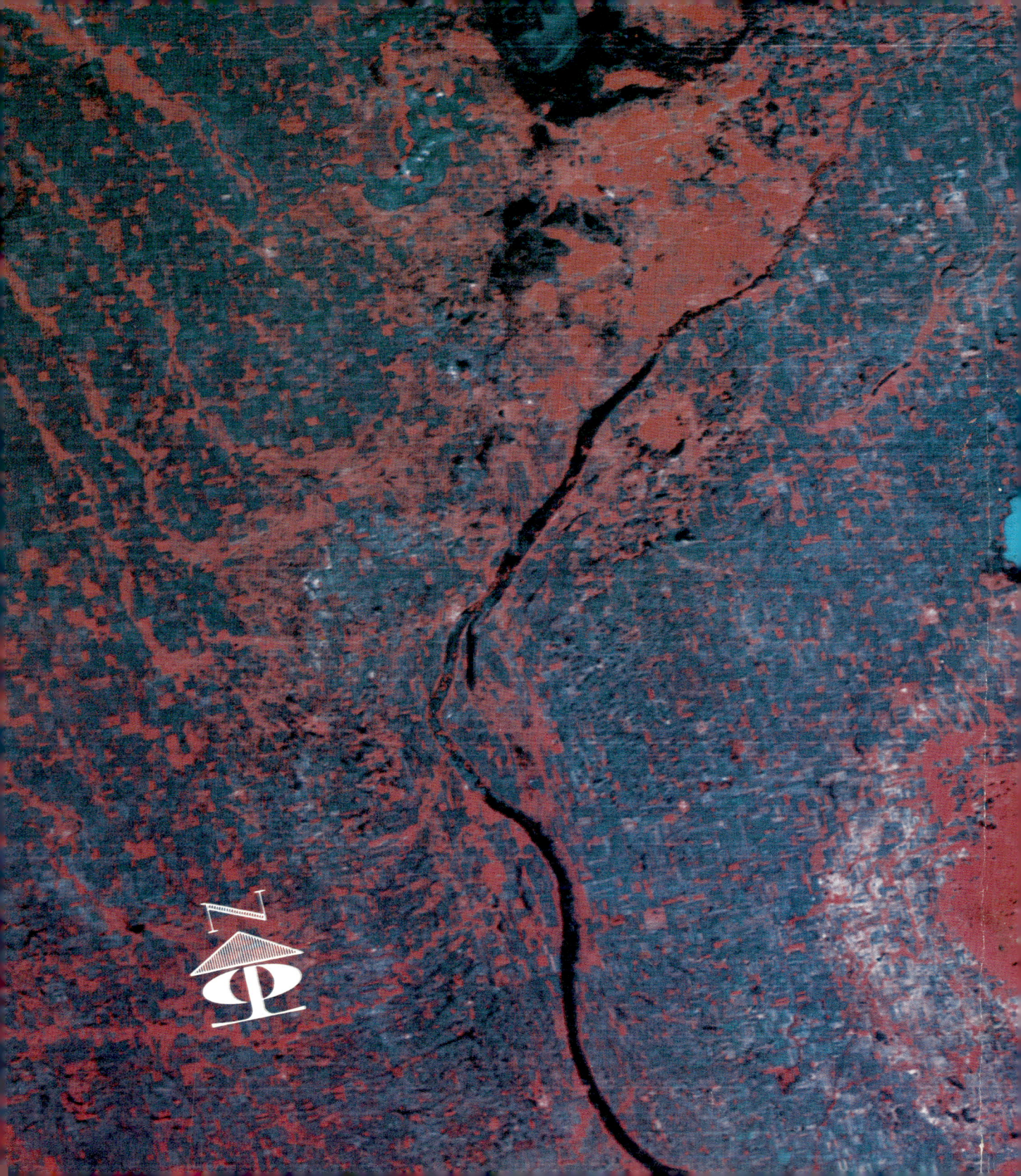

The New Enchantment of America
NORTH DAKOTA

By Allan Carpenter

CHILDRENS PRESS, CHICAGO

ACKNOWLEDGMENTS

For assistance in the preparation of the revised edition, the author thanks:
CATHY PECHTL, Travel Division, the State Highway Department.

American Airlines—Anne Vitaliano, Director of Public Relations; *Capitol Historical Society,* Washington, D.C.; *Newberry Library,* Chicago, Dr. Lawrence Towner, Director; *Northwestern University Library,* Evanston, Illinois; *United Airlines*—John P. Grember, Manager of Special Promotions; Joseph P. Hopkins, Manager, News Bureau; Carl Provorse, *Carpenter Publishing House.*

UNITED STATES GOVERNMENT AGENCIES: *Department of Agriculture*—Robert Hailstock, Jr., Photography Division, Office of Communication; Donald C. Schuhart, Information Division, Soil Conservation Service. *Army*—Doran Topolosky, Public Affairs Office, Chief of Engineers, Corps of Engineers. *Department of Interior*—Louis Churchville, Director of Communications; EROS Space Program—Phillis Wiepking, Community Affairs; Charles Withington, Geologist; Mrs. Ruth Herbert, Information Specialist; Bureau of Reclamation; National Park Service—Fred Bell and the individual sites; Fish and Wildlife Service—Bob Hines, Public Affairs Office. *Library of Congress*—Dr. Alan Fern, Director of the Department of Research; Sara Wallace, Director of Publications; Dr. Walter W. Ristow, Chief, Geography and Map Division; Herbert Sandborn, Exhibits Officer. *National Archives*—Dr. James B. Rhoads, Archivist of the United States; Albert Meisel, Assistant Archivist for Educational Programs; David Eggenberger, Publications Director; Bill Leary, Still Picture Reference; James Moore, Audio-Visual Archives. *United States Postal Service*—Herb Harris, Stamps Division.

For assistance in the preparation of the first edition, the author thanks:
William L. Guy, Governor; Flossie Perkins, Assistant Professor, University of North Dakota; North Dakota State Travel Department; and the Fargo Chamber of Commerce.

Illustrations on the preceding pages:
Cover photograph: Scoria Point, Sunset Storm, USDI, NPS, Theodore Roosevelt National Memorial Park
Page 1: Commemorative stamps of historic interest
Pages 2-3: Sunset in Central North Dakota, Travel Division, North Dakota State Highway Department
Page 3 (Map): USDI Geological Survey
Pages 4-5: Turtle Mountain Area, EROS Space Photo, USDI Geological Survey, EROS Data Center

Revised Edition Copyright © 1979 by Regensteiner Publishing Enterprises, Inc.
Copyright © 1968, Childrens Press
All rights reserved. Printed in the U.S.A.

3 4 5 6 7 8 9 10 11 12 R 85 84 83 82 81 80

Project Editor, Revised Edition:
  Joan Downing
Assistant Editor, Revised Edition
  Mary Reidy

Library of Congress Cataloging in Publication Data

Carpenter, John Allan, 1917-
  North Dakota.

  (His The new enchantment of America)
  1. North Dakota—Juvenile literature.
  I. Title. II. Series.
  F636.3.C3   1979   978.4   79-14470
  ISBN 0-516-04134-7

Contents

A TRUE STORY TO SET THE SCENE **9**
　North Dakota Breaks the News

LAY OF THE LAND.................................**11**
　Land of the Friendly Allies—Rivers and Lakes—Outstanding Features—
　In Ancient Times—Climate

FOOTSTEPS ON THE LAND..........................**21**
　Prehistoric Peoples—Many Tribes, Many Tongues—How the Indians
　Lived—Indian Skills—Customs and Legends—Coming of the Hideous
　Pale Skins—Sent by the Great White Father—An Active Winter—Going
　and Coming

YESTERDAY AND TODAY............................**35**
　Trappers, Traders, Settlers—War with the Sioux—Settlement Begins—
　Tragic News—A Settled State—The State in Business—A Modern State—
　The People of North Dakota

NATURAL TREASURES..............................**47**
　Land that Burns and Other Minerals—Tales of Gopher Tails and Other
　Animals—Birds and Fish—Growing Things

PEOPLE USE THEIR TREASURES.....................**53**
　Agriculture—Manufacturing and Mining—Transportation and Communication

HUMAN TREASURES................................**63**
　"The Strenuous Life"—The Marquis and the Meat Madness—Creative
　and Ingenious People—Such Interesting People

TEACHING AND LEARNING..........................**71**

ENCHANTMENT OF NORTH DAKOTA....................**73**
　Bismarck—Fargo—Other Cities—Other Points of Interest

HANDY REFERENCE SECTION........................**87**
　Instant Facts—You Have a Date with History—Thinkers, Doers,
　Fighters—Governors of the State of North Dakota

INDEX..**91**

PICTURE CREDITS................................**96**

ABOUT THE AUTHOR...............................**96**

A True Story to Set the Scene

NORTH DAKOTA BREAKS THE NEWS

"It was, for stark tragedy, horror and surprise, perhaps the greatest news story ever flashed over a telegraph wire to a stunned and stricken country, in the history of the United States." This was North Dakota poet laureate James W. Foley's description of one of the most unusual of the many stories of enchantment of North Dakota.

The story began in 1876 when the Seventh United States Cavalry jogged out of Fort Abraham Lincoln, near present-day Mandan and across the river from Bismarck. Banners flew and bands played as the gallant troops rode out from the fort, led by the dashing, foolhardy, and controversial George Armstrong Custer, his long blonde hair streaming from beneath his hat. To see him off, his wife rode on a short part of the journey.

That journey and its tragic results make up one of the most widely discussed episodes of American history.

In late June 1876, Grant Marsh, captain of the steamboat *Far West*, had tied his boat at the bank of the Big Horn River in south-central Montana, waiting word from the military commanders. He knew that the troops of Major Marcus Reno and of Custer were nearby, to the west. Custer had moved with extraordinary rapidity to meet the Indians, and the captain felt he must have reached the vicinity of the Little Big Horn River, not many miles from where the captain's boat was tied.

Suddenly a Crow Indian approached the boat; he could speak no English but squatted on the ground and began to draw in the sand with a pointed stick. First he placed a cluster of dots in the sand; pointing, he spoke the Crow word for "white men." Around these dots he drew a tight circle of other dots, which he called the Crow word for "Sioux." With a quick slash of his hand the Crow brushed away all the "white" dots. Captain Marsh understood this to mean that the troops had suffered a great disaster.

There were no survivors, of course, from Custer's immediate

command, but the wounded men from Major Reno's troops were brought to Captain Marsh's boat. When the last desperately wounded soldier was aboard, Captain Marsh headed for Bismarck. His record-breaking fifty-four-hour voyage under forced steam took him from the Big Horn into the Yellowstone River, through the wilderness to the Missouri River, and down the long reaches of the Missouri to Bismarck.

On a sultry night in early July, residents of Bismarck were awakened by the noise of shouts and the creaking of the wagons hurriedly brought up to take the wounded from the *Far West*. Bismarck was stunned by the news that 276 men had been killed. Twenty-six wives of the massacred men, including Mrs. Custer, wept at Fort Abraham Lincoln.

The *Bismarck Tribune* had sent a reporter, Mark Kellogg, with the Custer troops. He, too, was killed, but a buckskin pouch found on his body held many vital notes on the battle, and it was brought back to Bismarck by Captain Marsh. Colonel C.A. Lounsberry, founder and editor of the *Tribune,* wrote and published the story of the Custer disaster and scooped the entire journalism world with the account of what would become the best-known Indian battle in American history.

Colonel Lounsberry also made arrangements for the *New York Herald* to buy the story. While the telegraph wires were held open for twenty-four hours at an estimated cost of $3,000, Colonel Lounsberry sent out what James Foley called "perhaps the greatest news story ever flashed over a telegraph wire."

Thus the whole world learned of the tragedy, by way of North Dakota.

Lay of the Land

LAND OF THE FRIENDLY ALLIES

The word Dakota means "friends" or "allies" in the Sioux Indian language. Early explorers however, might have had their doubts about the friendliness of either the people or the land.

Because it lies about 1,500 miles (2,414 kilometers) from the Atlantic Ocean, from the Pacific Ocean, from the Arctic Ocean, and from the Gulf of Mexico—equally distant from all—geographers say that North Dakota is located in almost the exact center of the North American continent.

The state has three main physiographic regions: the low, flat bed of the Red River Valley, the Drift Prairie (sometimes called Drift Plains), and the Missouri Plateau.

The Red River Valley is not a true valley but rather the bed of an ancient lake. The portion in the United States extends 235 miles (378 kilometers) southward from the Canadian border. The North Dakota portion of the lake bed is approximately 35 miles (56 kilometers) wide and varies from 750 to 970 feet (229 to 296 meters) above sea level.

The western edge of the Red River Valley region is marked by a rise of 300 to 400 feet (91 to 122 meters) known as the Pembina Escarpment (more properly called the Manitoba Escarpment). West of this escarpment is the Drift Prairie, which extends to the Missouri Escarpment; it rises 300 to 500 feet (91 to 152 meters) above the Drift Prairie. Between this escarpment and the Missouri River lies the Altamont Moraine, a line of rough hills. From these hills to the Missouri River is an area called the Coteau du Missouri.

West and south of the Missouri River is the tremendous area known to local residents as the Slope, but more properly called the Missouri Plateau region. V-shaped valleys, buttes, and hills formed by erosion are found here.

Three states—Minnesota, South Dakota, and Montana—and two Canadian provinces—Saskatchewan and Manitoba—are North Dakota's neighbors. The long boundary line with Canada is arrow straight, as are the even longer boundary with South Dakota and the shorter boundary with Montana. Only the eastern boundary, following the Red River of the North and the Bois de Sioux River, is a naturally formed border.

RIVERS AND LAKES

Two great river systems drain North Dakota—the Red River of the North and the mighty Missouri River. The Red is formed where the Bois de Sioux and Ottertail rivers converge at Wahpeton. The Red's longest tributary in North Dakota is the Sheyenne. Another tributary of the Red, which surprisingly never runs into it in North Dakota, is the Souris. It drains into the Assiniboine in Canada, which meets the Red at Winnipeg, Manitoba. The Souris was named by French explorers who saw large numbers of field mice scampering along its banks and gave the river the French name meaning mouse.

The Wild Rice, Maple, Goose, Tongue Park, Forest, Turtle, Rush, and Pembina rivers are other tributaries of the Red.

The Sioux Indians called the Missouri the *Wakpa Rehanka,* or Elk River. The Mandan Indians knew it accurately as *Mata*—the dividing line between two parts of land. To the Hidatsa Indians it was *Anati*—navigable water filled with earth—certainly a humorously apt description of the muddy Missouri.

The strange twists, strong treacherous currents, and many hazards to navigation of the Missouri have long been notorious and have led to many comments. One newspaper said: "Of all the variable things in creation the most uncertain are the action of a jury, the state of a woman's mind, and the condition of the Missouri River."

George Fitch had a clever description: "There is only one river with a personality, a sense of humor, and a woman's caprice; a river that goes traveling sidewise, that interferes in politics, rearranges geography and dabbles in real estate; a river that plays hide-and-seek with you today, and tomorrow follows you around like a pet dog with a dynamite cracker tied to his tail. That river is the Missouri."

The greatest tributary of the Missouri is the Yellowstone. However, only a small portion of the Yellowstone flows within North Dakota's boundaries. Other Missouri River tributaries are the Little Missouri, Knife, Heart, and Cannonball.

The James River, another tributary of the Missouri, is even longer than the Yellowstone, although its volume of water is smaller. The James flows almost parallel to the Missouri for a total of 710 miles (1,143 kilometers) and finally reaches the Missouri on the southern boundary of South Dakota, after the larger river turns eastward. The James River is said to be the longest unnavigable river in the world.

Smaller rivers with familiar names are the Beaver, the largest tributary of the Little Missouri, Des Lacs, and Park rivers.

Wind Canyon on the Little Missouri River

The Red River at Fargo

A divide or watershed slashes diagonally across the state, from almost the northwest corner to a point on the southern boundary between the James and Wild Rice rivers, not far from the southeastern corner of the state. Waters falling to the north and east of this divide flow into the Red River and finally to Hudson Bay. Waters dropping on the south and west of the watershed flow into the Missouri and eventually to the Gulf of Mexico. Although the James and Sheyenne rivers are only a few miles apart in one area, they empty at points almost 2,000 miles (3,220 kilometers) apart.

A miracle came to central North Dakota in 1956; where once there was only baked-dry land, a great lake began to form behind what was then the largest rolled earth-filled dam in the world. Garrison Dam and Lake Sakakawea have meant much to western North Dakota. The 1,600-square-mile (4,144-square-kilometer) lake has 1,500 miles (2,414 kilometers) of shoreline.

Another artificial lake is Lake Oahe, which extends up the Missouri River into North Dakota from Oahe Dam, in South Dakota.

The new lakes help offset the loss of one-third of the state's lakes that dried up during the great drought of the 1930s. Many of these never again filled with water.

The largest natural body of water in North Dakota is Devils Lake. Its waters have a high salt content because it lies in a basin that does not drain to any of the oceans. Other natural lakes include Stump Lake (a salt lake), Lake Upsilon, upper and lower Des Lacs lakes, Lake Darling, Long Lake, Round Lake, Rush Lake, Horse Head Lake, Arrowwood Lake, and many others, principally in the northeast and east. Additional reservoirs include Lake Ashtabula, Jim Lake, Lake Tschida, and Sweet Briar Lake.

OUTSTANDING FEATURES

White Butte rises to 3,506 feet (1,069 meters), the highest elevation in the state. Near its top, solid rock cliffs tower perpendicularly from 50 to 100 feet (15 to 30 meters) above the grassy side slopes.

Three groups of rolling hills in North Dakota are known as mountains. The forested Pembina Mountains rise above the floor of the Red River Valley. The Turtle Mountains, near Rolla, are really the undulating crest of a plateau about 400 feet (122 meters) above the nearby countryside, about 70 miles (113 kilometers) in length. This plateau also is covered with woodlands. The Indians thought the shape of the plateau resembled their sacred turtle, and they gave the mountains that name. The Killdeer Mountains, near Killdeer, consist of only two high hills, with bases stretching for nearly 10 miles (16 kilometers) across the countryside and peaks about 600 feet (183 meters) above the surrounding area. To the Sioux they were *Tahkahokuty,* "the place where the deer is killed."

Perhaps the most notable single feature of North Dakota's landscape is a region called "hell with the fires out" by General Alfred H. Sully. This, of course, is the Badlands of North Dakota, which has been sculptured into fantastic shapes, mostly by the erosion power of the Little Missouri River as it snakes its way northward. General Sully was not quite right about the fires being out; several fires have burned for long periods in the lignite (brown coal) veins of the region.

The formation of the Badlands is explained by an interesting Sioux legend. At one time, the legend relates, the region was a beautiful, flat, fertile prairie where the Sioux lived in comfort until driven out by an enemy. They prayed to the Great Spirit for revenge, and suddenly all the powers of nature attacked the region: earthquakes, fires beneath the earth, even lightning. The land was converted into deeply cut gorges, and all vegetation was destroyed.

The North Dakota Badlands are different from other badland regions in the United States. In North Dakota the Badlands are actually hills of clay and stone carved and cut by water and wind, rather than eroded valleys.

IN ANCIENT TIMES

The many layers of rock, sand, and soil below the surface of most of North Dakota were laid down by seas that swept in during different geological periods. As the forces beneath the earth raised or lowered the land, the seas subsided and rose. It is thought that salt water or freshwater seas covered most of the state at least eleven times. The layers of sand and mud deposited during each period were covered by later layers until the great weight pressed the lower layers into sandstone, shale, and other materials. Underlying most of the state, except the Red River Valley, is the white or grayish Dakota sandstone.

Eventually the climate became colder, and the first of the ice ages began. Tremendous masses of ice pushed down from the even colder lands to the north and covered various parts of the state on four different occasions. Much of the present surface of North Dakota resulted from the action of these glaciers.

The prehistoric Missouri River had flowed north into Hudson Bay, but the Wisconsin glacier forced the river to turn aside and take a new course. The glacial action in turning the Missouri toward the Mississippi had much to do with the shaping of future history.

*Above: "Caprock" erosion, Theodore Roosevelt National Memorial Park.
Below: A section of the North Dakota Badlands near Medora.*

When the glaciers melted, they left behind tremendous quantities of water. Some water flowed away, creating huge prehistoric rivers, but much of it remained in cups of land or valleys carved by the glaciers. In other cases rivers formed into lakes behind natural dams, known as moraines, made up of sand, stone, and earth dumped by the glaciers. There were several of these large prehistoric lakes in North Dakota.

The largest prehistoric lake was Lake Agassiz. Its area was larger than that of the five Great Lakes. It was formed about ten thousand years ago and lasted for a thousand years. Hilly rises in the land indicate the former shores of Lake Agassiz. The western shore, near present-day Buffalo, is known as Herman Beach. The entire Red River Valley was covered by Lake Agassiz, and it is thought that the site of Fargo was at least 200 feet (61 meters) below the surface of the prehistoric lake. With an area of more than 110,000 square miles (284,900 square kilometers), Lake Agassiz extended far into Canada and Minnesota. Some remnant lakes remain in those regions—Lakes Manitoba, Winnipeg, Winnipegosis, and Lake of the Woods.

On the floor of the present Red River Valley, the prehistoric lake left a silt layer twenty or thirty feet (six to nine meters) deep. This silty soil, known as chernozem, is rich, black, and one of the most fertile in the world. In fact, the glaciers' greatest single legacy in North Dakota was the layers of fertile soil deposited over much of the state.

Other large prehistoric lakes covered much of the present state. Lake Dakota extended about as far north as present-day Oakes and south into what is now South Dakota. Prehistoric Lake Souris lay in the bend of the present Souris River and was drained into Lake Agassiz by the prehistoric Pembina River. Devils Lake is the remainder of still another prehistoric lake. The tremendous quantities of water that flowed down these ancient rivers as a result of the melting glaciers can hardly be imagined.

The earliest forms of animal life lived in the ancient seas that covered North Dakota. Shellfish that died over millions of years were compressed to form the many layers of limestone. Strange as it may seem, the climate of North Dakota was once tropical, and tropi-

This petrified tree stump is an ancient relic in the Theodore Roosevelt National Memorial Park.

cal plants and animals flourished in a junglelike atmosphere. The remains of the tropical trees and plants were pressed further and harder into the earth until over millions of years they were compressed into soft coal known as lignite. As the animals died over the eons, their remains were compressed into what is now petroleum and natural gas.

Fossil relics of ancient plants and animals may still be found in many parts of North Dakota. Some of the most impressive are the petrified forests and trees found in the Badlands and other areas. Outlines of prehistoric sequoia and cypress, and many kinds of shellfish are visible in many of the rocks and lignites of the state. Fossil bones of many ancient animals have been found. The White River fossil beds are noted for their many titanothere relics. Mammals, fish, turtles, and other reptile fossils have been discovered in abundance in the state.

CLIMATE

Because of its generally uniform land surface, North Dakota's climate is fairly similar throughout the state. At the very heart of the North American continent, North Dakota not surprisingly has what is known as a Continental climate. This type of climate is renowned for its tremendous range of temperature. An all-time high of 124°F. (51.1°C.) at Medora in 1912 is contrasted with the all-time low of -60°F. (-51.1°C.) at Parshall in 1936—a range of 184°F. (102°C.), wider than the range of Alaska and only slightly less than the range of Montana.

The extremes do not last long, however. The average summer temperature is 65° to 72°F. (18.3° to 22.2°C.), and the nights are cool. Winter extremes are somewhat modified by comparatively low humidity.

Annual average rainfall is 18 inches (45.7 centimeters), ranging from 22 inches (56 centimeters) in the southeastern corner to 14 inches (36 centimeters) in the southwestern corner. Most rainfall comes in late spring and summer.

Footsteps on the Land

PREHISTORIC PEOPLES

An early visitor to the site of present-day Fargo drank in the pleasant springtime surroundings, the nodding prairie blossoms, and the cloudflecked day. "It's a beautiful land," he wrote later, "but I doubt that human beings will ever live here."

His prediction may have been at least twenty thousand years too late, for there are indications that people have lived in the region for at least that long. Stone implements and tools of an unknown but very early age have been found in Bismarck and other areas.

Most of the mounds, pictographs (picture writing), such as those of Writing Rock State Park, and petroglyphs (picture carving) are probably considerably more recent, although many of them date back before the historic period.

Among the most interesting relics of the early peoples are the turtle effigies. These were crude outlines of turtles formed by rows of rocks. Who made them and what their purpose was is not known. Some experts believe they were placed to point the way to fresh water; others think they may have had something to do with religious observances.

Boulder rings, large rocks laid in circular form, are more common than the turtles. At one time it was thought that these were simply the tepee rings that were formed when rocks were placed around the bottom edge of the tepee covering to hold it in place. True tepee rings can be seen in many parts of the state. However, the boulder rings were placed on steep slopes and in many other places where it is unlikely that a tepee could have been pitched, so their meaning is also something of a mystery, although it is thought they were made about four hundred years ago.

Other evidence of prehistoric man, possibly in the period of a thousand years ago, is found in the flint quarries north of Hebron. Raw material was hacked out of rock for weapon points and tool handles. At one of the quarries on the Knife River there are more than three hundred pits. Here, using only crude tools, prehistoric men chipped out the ultrahard rock, leaving pits as much as 10 feet (3 meters) across and 5 feet (1.5 meters) deep.

MANY TRIBES, MANY TONGUES

The Indians found by the earliest European visitors in what is now North Dakota apparently had all moved into the region in comparatively recent times. Pushed out of their former homes by stronger groups, they migrated to safer living areas.

The Mandan were probably the first "modern" Indians to reach the territory. They moved slowly up the Missouri River and made villages in South Dakota. Later they built their main villages in the Heart River region where Mandan and Bismarck now stand. They seem to have lived here for many generations.

The Mandan were followed into what is now North Dakota by the Hidatsa and Cheyenne. The Hidatsa (also known as Gros Ventres or Big Bellies, or as Minnetaree or Absaroke) lived on the Missouri north of the Mandan; later they allied with the Mandan and the two tribes shared much of the same region. The Cheyenne made their home in the region of the big bend of the Sheyenne River, which takes its name from them.

In time another tribe, the Arikara, came into the area. The four tribes—Mandan, Hidatsa, Cheyenne, and Arikara—are known as agricultural tribes. They lived in permanent homes and villages and farmed as well as hunted for food.

Nomadic tribes with no permanent villages did not grow many crops, and they moved from place to place following the game and other food. The nomadic tribes of North Dakota were the Sioux, Assiniboin, and Chippewa. They also had most likely been driven into the the western regions from eastern areas.

All but three of the North Dakota tribes belong to the great Sioux language group. The Cheyenne and Chippewa are Algonquin and the Arikara are Caddoan.

The Sioux were probably the largest in numbers and were divided into seven major tribes—Yankton, Yanktonai, Mdweakanton,

Wahpekute, Wahpeton, Sisseton, and Teton. The Teton Sioux, living west of the Missouri River, were the largest Sioux branch and numbered more than half of the entire tribe. There were also seven tribal branches of the Teton Sioux.

HOW THE INDIANS LIVED

On spring days the women of the agricultural tribes prepared the soil and planted and cultivated their neat fields, where corn, squash, melons, pumpkins, beans, and sunflower seeds were the main crops. The Mandan people had a small-eared variety of corn that grew quickly enough to mature in the short summers.

The women also did most of the lodge building. These dwellings consisted of logs and poles chinked with earth. However, the men helped with the heaviest logs. For protection from enemies the lodges were usually built along the edge of a cliff or river. The unprotected side was fortified with a log wall and a ditch. The Mandan villages usually were designed with the lodges facing a central courtyard containing a hollow log known as the Big Canoe, the symbol of a legend in which the Mandan were saved from the great flood in a big canoe.

The flat roofs of the lodges in the agricultural towns provided places for the old men to watch for enemies, for sweethearts to court, and for people to gossip in the evening.

As with most of the North American Indians, the main duties of the men were hunting and protection of the tribe. Indian boys were taught the ways of war in make-believe battles.

The huge buffalo herds provided much of the food for both agricultural and nomadic tribes. Buffalo were extremely difficult to kill by stalking with a bow and arrow, so the Indians devised many ingenious ways of slaughtering them. They would build corrals of wood or brush, known as buffalo parks, and then drive the buffalo into these corrals. Generally there was a steep cliff or bank of a stream in the park, over which the terrorized buffalo would plunge and kill themselves. Almost every part of the buffalo was used. The

Artist George Catlin captured the fascinating Buffalo Dance, Mandan Village *(above) and the* Minnetaree Buffalo Hunt *(below).*

hides were especially prized for robes, and even the bone marrow was sewed into skin sacks and saved for winter use.

Another hunting activity was capturing eagles. The Indians would hide in pits, into which the eagles were decoyed with great cunning and captured. Eagle tail feathers were highly prized and very scarce, even in those days. In later periods one eagle tail feather might be traded for a pony. The feathers were used, of course, in the beautiful ceremonial headdresses passed on from generation to generation.

Until Spanish explorers came into what is now the southwestern and southeastern United States, the Indians were not familiar with horses. After the first horses were stolen by the Indians of those regions, the horse gradually made its way north until the tribes of North Dakota possessed large herds. The nomadic tribes were the best horsemen, ranking among the finest in the world.

Before the horses came, the only domestic animal was the dog, often kept as livestock by the Indians and highly prized for food. An early traveler once told of being served a fine meal by the Indians; just as he was enjoying his stew thoroughly one of the men said, "Dig deep; pup in bottom."

The tepees of the nomadic tribes were sometimes as much as twenty-five feet (almost eight meters) high. As many as fifteen buffalo hides were needed to wrap around the tent poles, which were placed in cone formation. About 15 feet (4.5 meters) across, each tepee was usually occupied by two families.

The nomadic tribes made more clothing than the agricultural peoples. In nomadic tribes, leather trousers, moccasins, and shirts frequently were worn by the men, who added buffalo robes in cold weather. Women wore decorated leggings and loose-fitting leather dresses, with moccasins, of course, for their feet.

A big fire in the center of the cluster of tepees was the scene for tribal councils. Here the boys also learned the history and legends of the tribe from the old men.

There was a good deal of variety in burial customs among the tribes, but an above-ground burial was common. Sometimes the bodies were placed in the branches of trees; at other times poles were arranged to form a kind of scaffold on which the body was placed.

William Clark described one of those scaffold graves: "an Indian woman ... had been raised about 6 feet, inclosed in Several robes tightly laced around her, with her dog Slays [sleighs or travois, an arrangement of poles pulled along the ground by dogs to carry freight], her bag of Different coloured earths paint, small bones of animals, beaver, nales and Several other little trinkets, also a blue jay, her dog was killed and lay near her."

INDIAN SKILLS

The Indians were often skilled in making excellent use of the materials on hand. Many women produced fine beadwork or other embroidery. Some of their pottery was cleverly made and often showed a good deal of artistry. Tanning and working with hides were developed to a real art. Even musical instruments were made.

Awls and needles made from bone or stone were virtually the only tools. Bound clusters of brush served as brooms. Flat stones or bones were bound to wooden handles for shovels and hoes. Corn was ground with a wooden pestle in a hollow post. For weapons, flint was quarried for arrow and spear heads; then came the tiresome process of chipping the points into shape with tempered bone tools. Unfinished points can still be found at the quarry in Crowley Flint Quarry State Park.

One of the most interesting products manufactured by the Indians was the bull boat. This was made by bending saplings into a rounded wooden frame. Over this was stretched a green buffalo hide, which in shrinking pulled itself tightly around the frame. This clumsy boat, like a big tub, almost never capsized and was extremely useful in treacherous, rough waters such as the Missouri River.

CUSTOMS AND LEGENDS

One of the most important places in a Mandan village was the ceremonial lodge. The one at Old Slant Village in Fort Abraham Lin-

Trial of Courage of the
Mandan Men, *by George Catlin.*

coln State Park was eighty-four feet (about twenty-six meters) across. Here various ceremonies of the tribe were held, including the initiation of boys into manhood. This rite included much bloody torture. At the feast of Keepa, men tortured themselves by hanging from skewers placed into the chest until the skewers pulled through the flesh. Many features of this feast were similar to the sun dances of other tribes.

The Mandan had a buffalo dance to invoke good luck in the buffalo hunt and a rain dance. It was said the rain dance was always

27

effective because it didn't end until the rain came, no matter how long that might be.

After the death of a member of the family, a Mandan would slash himself and mourn for a year. Often very costly sacrifices of property were made after the death of a loved one. For a long time after a death, the relatives would go to the graveyard and moan; the wailing sometimes could be heard for miles.

A major legendary hero of the Mandan is known as the Good Furred Robe. He is supposed to have instructed the Mandan in almost all of their skills.

The most sacred place of the Mandan nation was the Holy Hill of the Mandan. After the great flood, the legend says that the Indian ark rested on the top of this hill, and man and woman first came to earth there. The Sioux and Arikara also held the place in reverence, and even into modern times many were reluctant to approach the hill. Rocks on the hill have many petroglyphs, and there are numerous colorful pictographs.

The Sioux had two sacred rocks. One was shaped in the form of a woman, seated and holding her baby; the other is the Inyan Bosdata, a standing rock, near Hastings.

For the nomadic tribes, the year began and ended with the Sun Dance. The calendar was maintained by keeping a count of each winter. The tribe's wise man would review the events of each year and give the past year a name, such as No Summer. From that time on events of that year would be dated from the year of No Summer.

One of the interesting customs of the Sioux was carrying the babies in cradle boards. One moment a baby's board might be hanging on the limb of a tree, and the next it might be hooked to the cinch of a horse jogging across the prairie. Again, the cradle board might be strapped to the mother's back.

COMING OF THE HIDEOUS PALE SKINS

On the eastern bank of the Missouri opposite the mouth of the Cannonball River stood a Sioux village. In the village a medicine man woke one morning, according to legend, and told of a disturbing dream. He said he had seen a strange race of men with hideous pale skins marching relentlessly toward their lands and that these awful-looking people would some day take the land away from them.

Few visions have ever been so accurately prophetic. The long march of the people with the pale skins never ceased once it began, just as the old medicine man had foretold.

There has long been another legend in North Dakota that at least one crew of Norse sailors reached North American shores in their Viking boats and managed to come overland as far as the Red River Valley. No evidence ever has been found to prove such legends, but the story persisted in much of Scandinavia that such people founded a lost race of fair-haired, blue-eyed people, and that these descendants of Norse explorers lived in what is now North Dakota. Strangely, many of the Mandan Indians have something of a Caucasian look. The whole story appears to be nothing more than legend.

As early as 1682 France claimed the great region that included North Dakota, but for sixty years no emissary of the king of France appeared in the region. In 1738 Pierre Gaultier de Varennes, known as Sieur de La Vérendrye, came into what is now North Dakota on one of the many journeys made over the generations to find a route to the Orient. Vérendrye also sought new rich regions for trapping and fur trading. After setting up several trading posts in Canada, he decided to visit the Mandan tribes. He set out along the Pembina River and went past the Turtle Mountains, until he reached the Mandan village located near present-day Menoken. Vérendrye's sons accompanied him on the journey.

The Frenchmen presented the Mandan leaders with an impressive lead plate inscribed with the claim of the French king to the territory. A similar plate later left in South Dakota was rediscovered, but the North Dakota plate has never been found.

In 1742 Vérendrye's sons, Francois and Louis-Joseph, again passed through North Dakota on an exploration that took them as far as Montana.

The old Indian's nightmare about his land began to come true soon after the Vérendryes had visited the area. Smallpox and other diseases brought by the Europeans, for which the Indians had no immunity, began to take their toll of large numbers of Indians.

In 1762 Great Britain took over all French interests in Canada, and Spain received control of the Mississippi Valley, including most of present-day North Dakota.

There may have been occasional visitors to the region, but the next important expedition was that of David Thompson, the renowned British scientist, in 1797. In spite of the unusually severe winter, his party visited the Indians along much of the present boundary with Canada and dropped down to the Mandan towns on the Missouri. Information about the Indians that Thompson kept in his journal is one of the most revealing records of their life and work. In 1818, Thompson helped survey the Canadian-United States border.

Fur trader Charles Chaboillez set up the first trading post in what is now North Dakota in 1797. This was located a short distance south of Pembina. Chaboillez represented the North West Company; by 1801 the great Hudson's Bay and XY companies had also managed to set up trading posts in the area.

SENT BY THE GREAT WHITE FATHER

In 1803, the Louisiana Purchase placed most of North Dakota under United States control. In 1804, under the direction of Meriwether Lewis and William Clark, one of the greatest explorations of history worked its way up the Missouri River and entered what is now North Dakota on October 13.

This turned out to be the last day of the two-year expedition on which any member of the party had to be court-martialed and disciplined. Robert Frazier was sentenced to receive seventy-five lashes for insubordination. Clark wrote, in his own quaint style and spelling: "The punishment that day allarmed, the Indian Chief very much, he cried aloud (or effected to cry) I explained the Cause of the punishment and the necessity [for it] which he thought examples were also necessary, & he himself had made them by Death, his nation never whiped even their Children, from their burth."

Winter was nearing and the company had to make winter camp. They chose a spot about twelve miles (nineteen kilometers) up the river from present-day Washburn, near the main villages of the Mandan and Arikara. The Sioux had forced the Mandan to move farther north from the Bismarck area, where their headquarters had been for a long time.

Biddle, one of the Lewis and Clark party, wrote: "This latitude by observation is 47°21' 47", and the computed distance from the mouth of the Missouri is sixteen hundred miles. This place which we call Fort Mandan . . . two rows of huts or sheds, forming an angle, of 14 feet square and 7 feet high, with plank ceiling, and the roof slanting so as to form a loft above the rooms, the highest part of which is 18 feet from the ground." The cabins were made of logs, chinked with mud.

AN ACTIVE WINTER

Several French and Canadian trappers visited the region from Canadian trading posts farther north and east and gave the explorers information; Lewis and Clark went out with some of the war parties to help the Mandan against their enemies.

On Christmas day, Clark wrote: "I was awakened before Day by a discharge of 3 platoons from the Party and the french [boatmen], the men merrily disposed, I give them all a little Taffia [rum] and permited 3 Cannon fired, at raising Our flag, Some Men Went out to hunt & the others to danceing and continued untill 9 oclock P.M. when the frolick ended EC."

On the same day, Ordway, another of the party, noted ". . . we had the Best to eat that could be had & continued firing dancing & frolicking dureing the whole day. the Savages did not Trouble us as we had requested them not to come as it was a Great medicien day with us. We enjoyed a merry cristmas dureing the day & evening untill nine oClock—all in peace & quietness."

On New Year's Day, 1805, Clark wrote: ". . . we suffered 16 men with their Musik [fiddle, tambourine, and horn] to visit the 1st

Meriwether Lewis in frontiersman's garb. Painted by Saint-Mémin in 1806.

Village for the purpose of Danceing, by as they Said the perticular request of the Chief of that Village . . . I found them much pleased at the Danceing of our men . . . at night the party returned, with 3 robes, and 13 Strings of Corn which the indians had given them. The Day was worm, Themtr 34° above o, some fiew Drops of rain about Sunset, at Dark it began to Snow, and Snowed the greater part of the night."

Lewis and Clark met the great chief of the Mandans and his counterparts in the other tribes. They gave medals and gifts to the chiefs and other important persons. They also did their best to turn the fur and other trade toward the United States and to let the Indians know that their principal chief was now the president in Washington, D.C.

The expedition leaders offered much advice to the Indians. Their counsel on not going to war, as Clark described it, might well be heeded by modern leaders: "One of the 1st War Chiefs of the big bell[i]es [Gros Ventre] nation came to see us.... This War Chief... informed us of his intentions of going to War in the spring against the Snake Indians we advised him to look back at the number of Nations who had been distroyed by War, and reflect upon what he was about to do, observing if he wished the happiness of his nation, he would be at peace with all, that by being at peace and haveing plenty of goods amongst them & a free intercourse with those defenceless nations, they would get on easy tirms a greater Number of horses, and that Nation would increas, if he went to War against those Defenceless people, he would displease his great father, and he would not receive that pertection & care from him as other nations who listened to his word. This Chief who is a young man 26 ye. old replied that if his going to war against the Snake indians would be displeasing to us he would not go, he had horses enough."

GOING AND COMING

As the ice began to break up in the Missouri in the spring, the Lewis and Clark party made preparations to enter a region that no non-Indian had ever seen. Lewis's notes for April 7, 1805, read: "Having on this day at 4. p.m. completed every arrangement necessary for our departure, we dismissed the barge and crew with orders to return without loss of time to St. Louis."

The expedition's greatest accomplishment during the winter was gathering a tremendous amount of information about the country and learning as much as possible about the region to the west. The Minnetaree tribesmen provided the most and best information about the west.

The explorers sent back large quantities of plants and animals that were new or unusual, and the information about the Indian tribes sent back east was the most complete ever gathered on the Indians of the West. Their letters carried complete reports of other findings up to that time.

Leaving Fort Mandan for the west, Lewis was able to write: "... I could but esteem this moment of my departure as among the most happy of my life. The party are in excellent health and sperits, zealously attached to the enterprise and anxious to proceed; not a whisper or murmor of discontent to be heard among them, but all act in unison, and with the most perfict harmony."

With them were the hired interpreter, Toussaint Charbonneau, his little son, Pompey, and wife, Sacajawea, the Indian woman who became famous for her part in the journey.

One of the high points of the entire expedition was the first sight of the mighty Yellowstone River, the greatest tributary of the Missouri. Lewis wrote: ".... beliving that we were at no very great distance from the Yellow stone River, I determined to proceed by land ... proceeded about four miles ... I ascended the hills from whence I had a most pleasing view of the country, particularly of the wide and fertile vallies formed by the missouri and the yellowstone rivers ... [later] Capt Clark measured these rivers just above their confluence; found the bed of the Missouri 520 yards wide, the water occupying 330. it's channel deep. the yellowstone river including it's sandbar 858 yds, of which the water occupied 297 yards, the deepest part 12 feet."

Soon afterward they left the boundaries of what is now North Dakota and did not return until the next year. On the way back they visited for a time with their friends at Fort Mandan. The party carried a swivel cannon mounted on one of their boats; Lewis had it removed from the boat and "I then [with] a good deel of ceremony made a present of the swivel to the One Eye Chief, and told him when he fired this gun to remember the words of his great father which we had given him."

Taking their final leave, "we were accompd to the Canoes by all the village Maney of them Cried out aloud ... the chiefs informed that when we first came to their Country they did not beleive all we had Said but they were now convinced that everthing we had told them were true, that they should keep in memory every thing which we had said to them, and Strictly attend to our advice."

Lewis and Clark soon passed from North Dakota for the last time, but the results of their journey were to be remembered for all time.

Yesterday and Today

TRAPPERS, TRADERS, SETTLERS

In the early 1800s other explorers, naturalists, and military men visited the region, but the trappers and traders were the most active. Manuel Lisa opened a trading post near present-day Mannhaven. Historian Lewis Crawford wrote: "These were the true pathfinders, the true explorers, the heralds of empire." As more traders and trappers came into the West the competition for furs became stronger. The biggest competitors for furs were the Hudson's Bay and North West companies. Others were Sublette and Campbell, John Jacob Astor's American Fur Company, the Missouri Fur Company, and Northwestern Fur Company.

In order to make the best trades with the Indians, the fur traders had no regrets about giving them great quantities of liquor and keeping them almost constantly drunk.

In 1812 William Douglas, Earl of Selkirk, sponsored the first true settlement in what is now North Dakota. With permission of the Hudson's Bay Company, he sent a group of Scottish people who had been displaced from their own homes to farm near Pembina. The traders, however, wanted to get rid of them and did everything possible to make them leave. When the boundary survey revealed that they were actually in the United States, the Selkirk settlers moved north into Canada.

In 1828 the Astor American Fur Company established Fort Union on the Missouri River, just on the North Dakota side of today's boundary with Montana. For forty years this was the most important post in the whole vast northcentral region.

One of the worst epidemics in American history occurred in 1837. Smallpox ravaged the Indian villages, and many tribes lost more than half of their people.

One of the interesting expeditions of the period was made by Jean Nicollet and John C. Frémont. Among other activities, Frémont in 1839 named Lake Jessie in honor of his fiancée, Jessie Benton, daughter of Missouri Senator Thomas Hart Benton.

In 1845 Bartholomew Berthold established his trading post, Fort Berthold, near present-day Garrison.

The first fort built by the federal government in what is now North Dakota was Fort Abercrombie, constructed in 1857. Most of the present state was without settlement, with a few scattered trading posts and no formal government.

Dakota Territory was organized in 1861, with the family physician of President Abraham Lincoln, Dr. William Jayne, as its first governor. This territory covered both the Dakotas and parts of Montana and Wyoming. Its capital was Yankton, now in South Dakota.

WAR WITH THE SIOUX

The agricultural tribes were generally friendly to the settlers but the Sioux were always hostile. In 1862 the Sioux in Minnesota massacred settlers in a wide area and then fled into the Dakotas. On September 3, the Sioux attacked Fort Abercrombie on the banks of the Red River. When they failed to take the fort, they established a siege. Defenders of the fort had little ammunition and because they did not even have a stockade they hastily built a cordwood wall for protection. In spite of all difficulties, they withstood an attack by four hundred warriors until help finally came.

As quickly as he could, Minnesota Governor General Henry Hastings Sibley gathered an army of 4,000 men, supported by 800 horses, 1,350 mules, and 225 wagons, and followed the Sioux into North Dakota in June 1863. The Indians eluded him, but he finally caught up with a group at the Battle of Big Mound, near present-day Tappen. Other skirmishes followed. He set out for home in August.

General Alfred H. Sully had been sent to chastise the Sioux. The Battle of Killdeer Mountain occurred on July 28; on September 3, 1863, he met the Sioux again in the Battle of Whitestone Hill, near what is now Ellendale.

It is possible that the Sioux Indians who were engaged in these battles were not the same ones responsible for the troubles in Minnesota.

SETTLEMENT BEGINS

Some of Dakota Territory had been opened to settlement on January 1, 1863, but there was no rush of settlers. In fact, Indian ownership was recognized throughout most of the area. However, immigrants were passing through in increasing numbers. A string of forts across the land was begun to protect the travelers from the Sioux. Fort Union was bought from its private owners in 1866, and dismantled; its parts were used to build Fort Buford, an army outpost for twenty-five years. Other forts were constructed soon afterward.

A small agricultural settlement had been established at Pembina in

This Currier and Ives picture of a prairie hunter with Indians in pursuit is a graphic reminder of the hostilities between the Indians and the settlers.

1851, and it was the only farming community in North Dakota for almost twenty years. In 1868 Joseph Rolette, an early fur trader, was the first person in North Dakota to file for a homestead. There were no others until 1870. In that year the non-Indian population of what is now North Dakota was probably not more than five hundred.

In 1868, five thousand Sioux Indians gathered with representatives of the United States government for a peace conference. The Indians came to the conference largely because of the influence of pioneer Jesuit missionary Father Pierre Jean de Smet. Sioux medicine man and leader Sitting Bull told Father de Smet, "Move out the soldiers and stop the steamboats and we shall have peace." The conference led to a treaty at Laramie, Wyoming, in 1869 in which the government agreed to keep non-Indian settlers out of large areas of the Dakotas, Montana, and Wyoming.

TRAGIC NEWS

The gold rush in the Black Hills of South Dakota broke the 1869 treaty, and the Sioux with their allies went on the offensive. George Armstrong Custer, hero of the Civil War and many Indian battles, had been bivouacked since 1873 at Fort Abraham Lincoln with his famed Seventh Cavalry. Custer, and especially his popular wife, were the center of the social activities for which the fort was noted.

The Custers were especially popular in the social life of recently established Bismarck, near the fort. The coming of the first railroad (described in detail in a later section) had led to the beginning of several settlements. Bismarck had its start when railroad squatters began to occupy the area in 1871 and 1872. The first train arrived at Bismarck in 1873. The little community had its first boom when the Black Hills gold fields brought a steady procession of people, supplies, and gold over the newly established stage line leading from Bismarck's railhead to the gold fields.

To meet the Indian threat, Custer and his troops rode out of Fort Abraham Lincoln in 1876 to the terrible fate that is so well known today.

A reenactment of Custer and his Seventh Cavalry troops riding out of Fort Abraham Lincoln in 1876 on their way to the Little Big Horn River.

A SETTLED STATE

The undefeated Sioux forces did not wait for the government to take its revenge; they went north to Canada where they remained until 1881, when Sitting Bull and his forces came back and surrendered peaceably at Fort Buford. Most Sioux accepted life on the reservations.

With the coming of peace and the expansion of the railroads, North Dakota began to develop more rapidly. In the Red River Valley, owners assembled great acreages and started to farm the rich land. These huge spreads were known as bonanza farms. Oliver Dalrymple bought 100,000 acres (40,470 hectares) of railroad land at a low price due to the depression of 1873. By 1895, 65,000 acres (26,300 hectares) of this were under cultivation. Other operations, almost as large, made this an unusual period. The ranch lands, of course, had many examples of even larger spreads.

Ranching also developed rapidly in North Dakota. Homesteaders and other smaller farmers soon began to come in a steady stream, with the largest increase of settlement beginning after about 1885.

Although the Indian wars had ceased, the war with nature has never ended. One of the worst floods in Missouri River history swept over the territory in 1881. Droughts and insect plagues added to the troubles. Prairie fires were among the worst disasters. In 1886 a prairie fire in the Bottineau region engulfed 500 square miles (1,295 square kilometers).

As early as 1804 Lewis and Clark had witnessed a prairie fire, and Clark wrote: " ... the fire went with such velocity that it burnt to death a man & woman [Indian], who could not get to any place of

Currier and Ives picture of one of the Prairie Fires of the Great West.

Safty.... a boy half white was saved unhurt in the midst of the flaim, Those ignerent people say this boy was Saved by the Great Medison Speret because he was white. The couse of his being Saved was a Green buffalow Skin was thrown over him by his mother... the fire did not burn under the skin leaveing the grass round the boy... this fire passed our Camp last [night]... it went with great rapitidity and looked Tremendious."

A prairie fire of September 25, 1888, ravaged the entire area between Jamestown and LaMoure. A newspaper account read: "A heavy and smoke laden atmosphere and a sky streaked with a dull red reflection of burning grass proclaimed the fierce raging of prairie fires north, south and west of the city last night.... For at least 40 miles in width the fire burned off every vestige of grass unprotected by breaks. One could hardly recognize the charred land the next day. Thousands of bushels of grain were burned and many men lost all they had, grain, buildings and stock."

One of the worst natural tragedies was the terrible winter of 1887-1888, when many cattlemen lost all their stock, and few lost less than half of their animals.

In spite of many seeming setbacks, however, Dakota Territory was moving slowly ahead. In 1883, largely because of the influence of Alexander McKenzie of Bismarck, the territorial capital was moved from Yankton to Bismarck.

Yankton wanted to remain the capital, and the law setting up a commission to choose a new capital required the commission to organize and meet in Yankton. The commission hired a special railroad train at Sioux City, Iowa; as the train reached the Yankton city limits, the meeting was called to order, officers were elected, the commission was organized, and the meeting was adjourned before the train had passed the city limits, thus meeting the requirements. The commissioners then went on to investigate the other cities that wanted the capital, including Bismarck.

With the coming of the capital, the new capital city had its second boom. A real estate upsurge caused the price of land in Bismarck to soar; fortunes were made and lost as land prices skyrocketed and later crashed.

A cornerstone was laid for a capitol in 1883, and former President Ulysses S. Grant was among the notables—including Sitting Bull—at the ceremony. Grant was with a party that was on its way to celebrate the completion of the Northern Pacific Railroad. Grant was shown around Bismarck and greatly admired the apple trees of a young Bismarck matron. Looking at the trees with their plentiful, large red fruit, the former president remarked, "Magnificent, magnificent! I am surprised, wonderfully surprised." The lady's neighbors were almost as surprised as Grant. She had bought three bushels of apples at the store and tied them on her trees to give Grant a good impression of a country not noted for its apples.

The people were anxious for statehood, to remove the disadvantages of territorial status. For many years Congress was petitioned regularly to make Dakota Territory into two states. At last, on May 14, 1889, a convention was elected to convene at Bismarck on the Fourth of July to write a constitution for a new state. The resulting constitution was based on a constitutional model created by James Bradley Thayer of the Harvard Law School. It was six times the length of the federal constitution and had many innovative provisions.

On November 2, 1889, President Benjamin Harrison signed bills creating the two new states—North Dakota and South Dakota. The president covered the documents so that no one could see which one he signed first. Because of this it will never be known which of the two preceded the other. To be accurate, North Dakota must be listed as the thirty-ninth or fortieth state, along with South Dakota.

The first governor of the new state was John Miller, and the United States senators were Gilbert Pierce of Fargo and Lyman Casey of Jamestown. The first state legislature met at Bismarck on November 19, 1889.

THE STATE IN BUSINESS

At the time of statehood, North Dakota was developing steadily. Sod houses were replaced by frame or brick houses; towns and houses dotted the prairies; bonanza farms were worked with methods more advanced than those in the East; and schools, colleges, and universities were taking root.

As more counties were formed, the constant battles among various towns for possession of the county seats provided some of the most lively portions of the state's history.

Drought and depression plagued the state in the early 1890s. In this period the railroads held a powerful interest in the state; some experts felt that railroad policies dominated the state government.

During the war with Spain in 1898 the entire North Dakota National Guard volunteered, but the men could not all be given places. North Dakota soldiers took part in much of the fighting in the Philippines.

"Honest John" Burke, elected governor in 1906, was supported by Democrats and the new Progressive Republican group, and Burke's election brought modernization to North Dakota politics. Government regulations were increased, and state institutions and schools received greater support. The first child labor law was enacted in 1909. In 1963, John Burke's statue was placed in Statuary Hall of the United States Capitol as North Dakota's representative in the Hall of Fame.

For many years North Dakota farmers complained that they could not get fair treatment in handling and marketing their grain. Their discontent led to the formation of the Nonpartisan League in 1915. Its program called for state ownership of terminal elevators, flour mills, packinghouses, and cold storage plants; state inspection of grain and grain docks; exemption of farm improvements from taxes; hail insurance issued by the state on an acreage basis; and banks for low-cost rural credit. With widespread promotion by A.C Townley, the Nonpartisan movement spread, mostly within the Republican party, and in 1916 Lynn J. Frazier was the first governor elected with the league's support.

World War I found 31,269 North Dakota residents in service; 1,305 lost their lives.

By 1919 North Dakota was ready for a unique experiment in United States history. The state entered business and finance as no state has done before or since. The North Dakota Mill and an Elevator Association was set up; a mill was bought at Drake and an elevator and mill built at Grand Forks; and the Bank of North Dakota was organized. Other state business enterprises soon followed.

However, by 1921 charges of mismanagement and excessive spending brought another historical development. For the first time in the United States, a governor (Lynn Frazier) was removed from office by the voting process known as recall. However, much of the program of state business and finance was continued, and North Dakota is today the only state operating in several commercial fields.

A MODERN STATE

In the 1930s the Great Depression and the worst drought in history brought great hardships to the state. The state capitol was destroyed by fire in 1930. Crop prices were so low that farmers could not keep up with their mortgage payments; so many foreclosures were threatened that Governor William Langer prohibited foreclosures for a time and also kept farm products from being shipped from the state with the hope that prices might increase.

A strange and confused period followed. Governor Langer was removed from office in 1934 by the North Dakota Supreme Court because of a former conviction for improper solicitation of contributions. This conviction was later overruled. Lieutenant Governor Ole Olson filled the remainder of Langer's term. Thomas H. Moodie took office as governor in 1935, and the state supreme court said his residence in the state did not meet requirements, and he was removed. Lieutenant Governor Walter Welford became the fourth governor of North Dakota in a period of about six months.

The people declared their confidence in Governor Langer by reelecting him in 1936. According to several authorities, he became the first governor in the United States to be elected without major party support.

With the assistance of the federal government and slow improvement throughout the country, the state gradually overcame the effects of the depression. One of the interesting recovery projects was the Subsistence Homestead Project of the North Dakota Rural Rehabilition Corporation. This included a model village at Burlington to aid miners who had been displaced at lignite mines.

World War II found 60,016 from North Dakota in service, and 1,939 gave their lives.

During the late 1940s the state experienced a period of prosperity never before equaled in its history, with ideal conditions both for growing and selling farm crops.

The discovery of high-grade oil between Minot and Williston in 1951 added new dimensions to the state's economy.

Much of the recent history of North Dakota has been concerned with the important and rapid economic development of the state, a large part of it sponsored by the state Economic Development Commission, established in 1957. The first large petroleum refinery in North Dakota was dedicated at Mandan in 1954. Uranium recovery from ore-rich lignite beds in the southwest began in 1963.

During the 1970s, environmentalists were increasingly concerned by expanding strip mining of coal in the western area. This was taking place because of the energy crisis. The Omega All-Weather Navigation System was completed near LaMoure in 1973, one of the few of its type anywhere. The state legislature adopted the Equal Rights Amendment in 1975, and the late 1970s saw the completion of one of the great irrigation systems of the land—with 2,000 miles (3,219 kilometers) of canals providing water for 1 million acres (404,686 hectares).

THE PEOPLE OF NORTH DAKOTA

Citizens of more than forty-two nations have come to North Dakota to make their homes. The largest number immigrated from the Scandinavian countries. Of these, the biggest group is those of Norwegian background. There are many of Swedish and Finnish background as well. Even little Iceland is well represented in North Dakota, in such communities as Mountain.

Canadians and their descendants, especially French-Canadians, form one of the largest groups of foreign born. German residents are numerous in Bismarck and other locations.

Ukranians at Wilton, Syrians from Damascus at Ross, where they have a mosque, and many other nationalities have enriched the culture and economy of the state.

The black population of North Dakota, only 777 at the time of the 1960 census, is now estimated at about 3,000.

The number of Indians in North Dakota in the 1970s was estimated at about fifteen thousand. Many, of course, no longer live on the reservations. For those who remain there are five reservations: Fort Berthold, Turtle Mountain, Fort Totten, Sisseton, and Standing Rock.

The first formal church services in North Dakota were held at Pembina in 1818 by Father Joseph Dumoulin, Father Joseph Provencher, and William Edge. In 1848 the Pembina mission was reopened by Father George Belcourt, who also opened another mission in the Pembina Mountains. He was even able to establish a small flour mill at Pembina. That same year, a Presbyterian minister, the Reverend Alonzo Barnard, brought the first Protestant services to North Dakota. However, services of both Catholics and Protestants were infrequent until 1871, when the Presbyterians sent Oscar H. Elmer throughout the Red River Valley to conduct services.

In summarizing the character of North Dakota people, North Dakota booster William P. "Bill" Sebens once asserted that North Dakota folk are the "greatest people I ever saw for taking a chance." Undoubtedly in years to come the state will continue to demonstrate that quality as it has in the past, to its own benefit.

Natural Treasures

LAND THAT BURNS AND OTHER MINERALS

"... the bluff is now on fire and throws out considerable quantities of smoke which has a strong sulphurious smell." In this way Meriwether Lewis called attention to one of North Dakota's natural resources. He was referring to a burning vein of lignite, a soft brownish type of coal, that probably had been ignited by an Indian campfire.

For centuries many of these lignite veins have caught fire and amazed or frightened natives and visitors. Early European explorers thought they were volcanoes. Some have burned for many generations.

Lignite lies under the whole western portion of North Dakota—28,000 square miles (72,520 square kilometers)—and the state possesses 64 percent of all the country's lignite. The reserve is estimated to contain from 400 to 600 billion tons (363 to 544 billion metric tons), enough to supply all of America's fuel needs for many generations. This is considered to be the largest single concentration of solid fuel in the world and is probably one of the most valuable minerals of the state.

The state's reserves of petroleum are estimated at 173 million cubic feet (about 5 million cubic meters) and natural gas reserves are thought to be 448 billion cubic feet (12.7 billion cubic meters). North Dakota ranks fourteenth among all the states in proven petroleum reserves. Among other North Dakota minerals are a wide variety of valuable clays, marl, mineral earth pigment, fuller's earth, bentonite, and cement rocks. Sodium sulphate, also known as glauber's salts, is found in only a few other places outside North Dakota.

Rock and gem hunters find the state a paradise. Agates are plentiful along the ancient Lake Agassiz beaches near Fargo and Grand Forks. Central North Dakota is noted for its moss agates, the Badlands for agatized wood. Other petrified wood, the beautiful milky blue opal, and scoria are gem hunters' prizes. Scoria is formed when sediments are baked and fused above burning beds of lignite coal.

Once numerous, prairie dogs today appear to be facing extinction.

According to some experts, the reserves of ground and surface water and the rich soil are North Dakota's greatest assets. The soil of the Red River Valley is compared for richness with that of the famous Nile River Valley in Egypt.

TALES OF GOPHER TAILS AND OTHER ANIMALS

The gopher, or flickertail, gives North Dakota one of its nicknames—Flickertail State. The story is told that in pioneer days church wardens often found gopher tails in the collection plates. Those who had no cash knew that the bounty of three cents each on gopher tails could be collected by the church.

Of the other smaller animals, the prairie dog was probably the most numerous. The mounds and burrows of prairie dog towns could be seen extending across the prairie for miles in the early days, housing untold millions of the little burrowers. Today, they appear to be facing extinction.

The first explorers found tremendous herds of large animals, including deer, elk, bighorn sheep, and especially buffalo. One early traveler estimated that a single buffalo herd contained two or three million of the formidable beasts. The grasslands were described as "black with buffalo."

As many as three thousand Indians gathered to hunt the buffalo in 1810 at what is now Wahpeton. The great Pembina buffalo hunts were known throughout the world. The white and Metis (mixed blood) hunters gathered at Pembina and sometimes extended the hunt as far as Fort Union. In the 1840 Pembina hunt, 1,630 people took part, using 1,210 ox carts to bring back more than 1 million pounds (453,600 kilograms) of buffalo meat. At one time in early North Dakota, almost everyone owned a buffalo robe, which were said to be the only real protection while traveling by wagon or carriage across the Dakota prairies in the icy winter.

Though the great buffalo herds are now gone and the animals once were hunted almost to extinction, some small protected herds remain.

A coyote at Lake Sakakawea, near Garrison Dam.

By the time young Theodore Roosevelt came to North Dakota the great buffalo herds were gone, but Roosevelt's books are full of the joy of hunting the remaining buffalo, as well as antelope, elk, mountain sheep, wolf, coyote, and the fearsome grizzly bear.

Lewis and Clark had many encounters with the grizzly; as Lewis wrote on April 13, 1805: "we also saw many tracks of the white [grizzly] bear of enormous size, along the river shore and about the carcases of the buffaloe ... the Indians give a very formidable account of the strength and ferocity of this anamal, which they never dare to attack but in parties of six eight or ten persons; and are even then frequently defeated with the loss of one or more of their party.... this anamal is said more frequently to attack a man on meeting with him, than to flee from him.... When the Indians are about to go in quest of the white bear, previous to their departure, they paint themselves and perform all those supersticious rights commonly observed when they are about to make war upon a neighboring nation."

Sadly, the grizzly bear is almost extinct today. It is seen only very infrequently in the highest and wildest parts of the nation. In North Dakota, bobcats and coyotes may still be seen, but only rarely. The beaver and otter that once provided riches for many fur companies are no longer abundant.

However, there is still widespread sport hunting available in North Dakota. White tail deer are found throughout the state, mule deer in the southwest, and antelope in the west and southwest.

BIRDS AND FISH

More than ten million migratory fowl, including varieties of ducks and geese, pass over North Dakota on their annual spring and fall migrations. Pheasant are plentiful in the south and southcentral regions. Sharptail grouse are found all over the state, but principally in the western two thirds, ruffed grouse generally in the northeast, and sage grouse in the far southwest corner. Even the wild turkey and Hungarian partridge are found in some parts of the state.

Nongame birds, surprisingly, include the pelican, and Arrowwood Lake has one of the most important feeding grounds for pelicans. The Arrowwood Wildlife Refuge is also maintained there.

Other important natural conservation areas in North Dakota are Sullys Hills National Game Preserve, where birds and animals are protected as well as a small buffalo herd, and the Souris Loop Refuges, known to naturalists as an area of great bird production and variety.

Although North Dakota is not usually thought of as a setting for bird life, more than three hundred species of birds are found in the state. One of the most charming is the Dakota song sparrow. Another somewhat unusual bird is the black-billed cuckoo. Even more unique is the burrowing owl, which finds homes in the deserted burrows of foxes, gophers, badgers, and other underground dwellers.

About sixty species of fish live in the waters of the state, and fishing is a major tourist attraction. The world's largest sauger was taken from the tailrace of Garrison Dam. Northern pike, trout, walleyed pike, bass, muskies, catfish, sturgeon, and many varieties of panfish are the major catches.

GROWING THINGS

In the spring the drab prairies brighten with a surprising variety of bloom. Three varieties of North Dakota's state flower—the delicate wild rose—color the roadsides in June. The blooms appear on plants that grow from 1 foot to 5 feet (30 to 152 centimeters) tall.

The all too common sunflower sometimes becomes a pest in grain fields, but its yellow blossom does much to brighten the landscape. Its seeds have many uses; the giant type has seeds that provide a rich cooking oil. The fleabane, perennial clover, and gaillardia are other welcome blossoms of North Dakota. Prickly pear cactus may be seen, as well as the unusual scoria lily, which opens its blooms only after the sun has gone down.

If North Dakota farmers were to vote on the most unpopular plant, it undoubtedly would be the pesky Russian thistle, which has plagued farmers and gardeners ever since its introduction.

Wild fruits include wild grapes and plums, chokecherries, juneberries, and the highbush cranberry.

The only forests that blanketed North Dakota in its natural state were on the Turtle Mountains near Bottineau and a few other high areas. Today, however, statewide tree-planting programs have resulted in large groves and long rows of trees to hold the soil during wind storms. Thanks to the plantings in cities and towns, most communities are now tree shaded, where once no leafy shadows were cast.

Among the unusual trees of North Dakota are the world's only columnar cedars.

Since the 1930s, conservation of the state's natural resources has been one of the most important considerations in North Dakota. Conservation of the soil and soil resources to prevent erosion, preservation of natural resources, flood control, prevention of damage to dams and reservoirs, assistance in maintaining the navigability of rivers, and preservation of wildlife are all state policy. The State Soil Conservation Committee, State Game and Fish Commission, and State Water Conservation Commission function in cooperation with similar federal agencies.

People Use Their Treasures

The major industries in North Dakota are agriculture (crops and livestock), minerals, manufacturing, and tourism.

AGRICULTURE

Someone has said that the soil of North Dakota is so rich that if a nail were stuck in the ground in the evening, by morning it will have grown into a crowbar. Economist Stuart Chase called North Dakota the "richest farming region of the world." It was the richness of the soil in the Red River Valley that brought the state's first great surge in agriculture—the huge crop farms known as bonanza farms. Most of these were broken up later into smaller units, but now the tendency again is for larger and larger farms, because one person can handle larger acreages with mechanized equipment, although farm helpers are almost impossible to find.

An eastern North Dakota farm.

Today the farmer can seed forty- or fifty-foot-wide (twelve- or fifteen- meter) strips at a time. When the grain is ripe, combines move across the waving grain like "steamers on a sunlit sea." If a North Dakota farmer can't find a machine to do a particular task, he is likely to invent it.

At the present time, 93 percent of the land in North Dakota is used for farming or ranching. In areas where rainfall is not sufficient, vast irrigation projects have been completed or are under construction to water the land for crops.

The state is divided into three agricultural belts. The Red River Valley and Drift Prairie make up the black earth farming belt, the Coteau du Missouri forms the farming-grazing belt, and the Missouri Slope is devoted to grazing and forage.

Wheat, of course, is king of crops in North Dakota; the state is second in total wheat production and ranks first among all the states in spring wheat. Three-fourths of all the hard, or durum, wheat grown in the United States comes from North Dakota. This is the type of wheat used in macaroni and similar foods. So much wheat pours from the Red River Valley that it is known by some as "the breadbasket of the world."

North Dakota has two other notable agricultural firsts. It leads the nation in both rye and flax. Only one other state grows more barley and wild hay. Sweet clover seed, crested wheat grass seed, oats, Kentucky bluegrass seed, potatoes, smooth bromegrass seed, sugar beets, corn for silage, and dry field beans are other crops.

Livestock, of course, has an important part, with cattle and calves ranking second to wheat in producing farm income. Income from livestock in North Dakota is more than $300 million.

The total income from all agriculture in North Dakota is about $2.5 billion.

MANUFACTURING AND MINING

Much of the manfacturing in North Dakota is based on processing farm and ranch products. The Marquis de Mores established the first

Above: Fargo Industrial Park. Industry in the state is small but growing.

meat packing plant in North Dakota at Medora, but the effort failed. Today, however, meat packing is a successful industry in the state.

It is not surprising that with so much wheat, one of the best-known names in wheat products—Cream of Wheat—originated at Grand Forks. The company's operations were later moved to Minnesota.

Another important processing operation is the dehydrating of alfalfa, most of which is used in mixed stock feeding.

The value of manufactured products in North Dakota—about $200 million—is among the lowest in the nation. However, North Dakota has made a strong and continuing effort to bring more manufacturing to the state. As a result, the state's industrial growth rate ranks among the highest in the United States.

It is interesting to note that North Dakota still operates a number of state businesses—a mill and elevator at Grand Forks and a state bank at Bismarck.

Much of the state is under lease to oil and gas operators or speculators. The latest figures show that twenty million barrels of liquid petroleum were produced from fourteen hundred wells.

Natural gas is processed at Tioga in a plant with a capacity to convert 65 million cubic feet (1.8 million cubic meters) of gas daily to butane, propane, and gasoline. Other plants are at McGregor and Lignite.

North Dakota's most abundant mineral, lignite, is being used more and more, and the state has a large and continuing research program to find new and better uses for lignite. A process for converting lignite into briquettes was perfected at the School of Mines of the University of North Dakota. This produces a fuel that burns like charcoal with an intense blue flame. Briquette plants in the state process this fuel, which is especially fine for fireplaces.

The Division of Mines and Mining Experiments conducts its lignite research jointly with the United States Bureau of Mines. A process has been developed that produces activated carbon from lignite. Lignite is also used in the production of a coloring material known as Van Dyke brown. About 50 percent of the domestic supply of Van Dyke brown is processed at Bowman.

Bentonite clay, mined in North Dakota, is used as an acid-activated bleaching agent, an oil-drilling mud, a bonding agent for heat and sound insulation blocks, and as a suspending, spreading, and adhesive agent in horticultural sprays and insecticides. It also is used as a mineral filter. Other clays are used for a range of products, from common brick to fine pottery. Fuller's earth is useful in decolorizing oils and fats, in refining mineral oil, in insecticides, as rotary-drilling muds, and for absorbents.

Opposite: Lignite (brown coal) mining in the state is done in an orderly fashion (top). When mining operations have been completed in an area, the land is restored and used for agricultural purposes (bottom).

Clinker, or scoria, found by the millions of tons in North Dakota, is used for track ballast, highway base material, sidewalks, and roads.

The total value of mineral production in North Dakota is more than $150 million.

TRANSPORTATION AND COMMUNICATION

Some of the most interesting and romantic events in North Dakota have been connected with steamboating on the Missouri and Red rivers. The first steamboat, the *Yellowstone,* reached the upper Missouri River in 1832. As the clumsy looking boat made its way upstream, Indians along the shore shot their dogs and horses as sacrifices to appease the gods who were sending such an awful creature to destroy them. Later, their name for a steamboat was "big medicine canoe with eyes."

Steamers on the Missouri could penetrate farther into the heart of the continent than other forms of heavy transportation. The Missouri was treacherous, with changing channels, sandbars, snags, and other dangers, including the Indians. At one time merchandise owed to the Indians from the federal government was improperly held aboard the steamer *Robert Campbell* by the Indian agent. The Indians followed the steamer along the banks for 600 miles (966 kilometers) demanding their goods. Several on both sides were killed in clashes.

Steamboat pilots needed such skill and courage that they could command salaries of $1,000 a month, an astronomical figure in those days.

One of the greatest steamboat obstacles was sandbars. Captain Grant Marsh described the usual manner of getting a boat off: "When she became lodged on a bar, the spars [long heavy poles like telephone poles] were raised and set in the river bottom like posts, their tops inclined somewhat toward the bow. Above the line of the deck each was rigged with a tackle-block over which a manila cable was passed, one end being fastened to the gunwale of the boat and the other end wound around the capstan. As the capstan was turned

Suspicious Indians on the banks of the Missouri River near Fort Berthold watch as a "fire canoe" passes by.

and the paddlewheel revolved, the boat was thus lifted and pushed forward. Then the spars were re-set farther ahead and the process repeated until the boat was at last literally lifted over the bar. From the grotesque resemblance to a grasshopper which the craft bore when her spars were set, and from the fact that she might be said to move forward in a series of hops, the practice came to be called 'grasshoppering.'"

Because of the large amount of wood needed to power a steamboat, there were many fueling stops along the way. Both Indians and non-Indians operated fueling stations. Cedar made a very valuable fuel, and some river men told how the Indians would color the ends of cottonwood red to resemble cedar. From midstream a steamboat captain would see what he thought was a pile of cedar. When he reached shore, he often bought the cottonwood rather than make another stop.

Tremendous quantities of goods and large numbers of passengers were carried on steamboats on the Missouri, including much of the gold of Montana and the Black Hills of South Dakota.

The first steamboat on the Red River was the *Anson Northrup*. Before the coming of steamboats, barges, scows, and smaller boats served for transport on both the Missouri and the Red. The steamboating boom on the Red River hit its peak in the 1870s. Then, as the river's level continued to fall, flourishing towns were left high and dry. When the river dropped in 1872, Frog Point (Belmont) became the head of navigation and was a thriving river port until another drop in water level forced the head of navigation downsteam; Belmont became a ghost town.

Fargo was also a center of steamboat construction at one time, and the profits to be made on the Red River steamboat runs were astoundingly high. The profit on one eight-day trip on the river was said to have been enough to pay for the cost of building the boat, as well as the three barges towed behind it.

A navigation company was even organized in 1879 for the very shallow James River. One newspaper wrote: "The craft is composed of a steam whistle, an engine the size of a teakettle, and a little boat under it." The effort was never successful.

The arrival of the railroads heralded the beginning of the end for steamboat transportation. Railroad surveys were conducted in the area as early as 1853. The Northern Pacific Railroad reached the Red River at Moorhead, Minnesota, in 1871; by the next year it had advanced to Fargo, and the first train reached Bismarck on June 5, 1873. The announcement of the coming of the railroad brought the first real boom to the Red River Valley. Rapid settlement of North Dakota did not begin until the railroads could carry settlers in and haul away the products of their farms. As the railroads advanced across the prairies, the North Dakota "landmark" — the grain elevator—sprang up beside them; at last the grains of the prairie farms could be moved to the world markets.

Among history's most picturesque modes of transportation was the Red River oxcart. These were two-wheeled vehicles of the simplest construction. Their axles were never lubricated, and the resulting squeak could be heard for miles over the prairie. Sometimes an oxcart train would consist of as many as fifteen-hundred carts, as the procession followed the tedious trail from Minneapolis to Winnipeg.

Faster overland transportation for passengers and light freight was provided by stagecoaches, with wagons carrying the heavy loads. The Bismarck—Deadwood (South Dakota) trail was among the most famous. At the stagecoach stops, the traveler might find a log cabin, roofed with sod or weed thatch; with luck there would be a window as well as a door. For fifty cents he or she could sleep on the dirt floor and buy a meal for another half dollar.

Today's overland travel in North Dakota offers two interstate highways—94 and 29—and numerous United States routes. The longest stretch of highway in the United States without a curve extends along North Dakota 46 from U.S. 81 to N.D. 30, a distance of 110 miles (177 kilometers), without a single bend.

The *Frontier Scout* is usually considered the first newspaper published in the state. It appeared first at Fort Union in July 1864 and was later moved to Fort Rice. The oldest continuously published newspaper in the state is the *Bismarck Tribune,* established July 11, 1873. Between 1864 and 1889, when North Dakota became a state, the surprising number of 125 newspapers had been established.

Tourism is a growing and important business in North Dakota, with millions of tourists flocking to the state.

Human Treasures

"THE STRENUOUS LIFE"

"That fool Joe Ferris says Roosevelt is going to be president," a Medora man was heard to exclaim disgustedly in 1884. The name of Joe Ferris has never gone down in history, but he probably should be remembered as a highly successful prophet, and perhaps as the first man to predict that Theodore Roosevelt would one day become president of the United States.

Few people would have been willing to make such a prediction when the young Roosevelt (twenty-five years old) arrived at Little Missouri (now Medora) in 1883. He was not a very healthy or prepossessing figure. From a wealthy and aristocratic family, Roosevelt had already done some writing and had served a term in the New York State Assembly. After both parents and his wife died within a short time, he moved to North Dakota in the hope that outdoor life there would help him regain his spirits and health.

The Westerners were inclined to make fun of this "dude from New York," who wore fashionable city clothes and needed heavy glasses. They called him "four eyes," with a not very complimentary inflection, until one night he knocked out a bully with his bare hands and took away his gun. Then the nickname became Old Four Eyes, with a note of admiration.

Roosevelt killed his first grizzly bear and his first buffalo on the Little Missouri River near present-day Marmarth on the Little Beaver River. He was so taken with hunting and other attractions of North Dakota that he purchased two ranches near Medora and made his home in a rough but comfortable cabin on his Chimney Butte ranch, and later at his Elkhorn Ranch thirty-five miles (fifty-six kilometers) down river. In the rugged duties of running cattle, in holding his own with the "tough hombres" of the West, and in all the other activities of the great outdoors, Theodore Roosevelt

Opposite: Statue of Theodore Roosevelt as a Rough Rider.

learned to live a strenuous life, and the Strenuous Life became the true theme of his existence from that time on. Later he recorded much of the life of frontier North Dakota in his fascinating book *Ranch Life and the Hunting Trail.*

One adventure occurred when three men stole one of the boats from his Elkhorn Ranch. Roosevelt and three ranch hands followed the thieves on a lively and exhausting three-day chase before capturing them. Sending his men home, Roosevelt herded the three captives to Dickinson and charged two of them with theft. The third was an older man. Roosevelt said he was the "kind of person who was not capable of doing either much good or harm." The elderly thief was tremendously grateful when Roosevelt did not press charges, and Roosevelt said it was the first time he had ever received thanks for labeling anyone a fool.

Roosevelt liked his neighbors and they liked him. They made him chairman of the local stockmen's association, and he quickly became a public figure, as this quotation from the *Dickinson Press* indicates: "The first Fourth of July celebration attempted in Dickinson took place last Monday. It exceeded the anticipation of all and proved to be a grand success—a day that will long be remembered. The day dawned bright and cool. Early in the morning people began to arrive and by ten o'clock the largest crowd ever assembled in Stark County lined the principal streets. The train from the west brought a number of Medora people. Amongst them was Hon. Theodore Roosevelt, the orator of the day. The celebration consisted of: A Parade, Addresses by Hon. Theodore Roosevelt and Hon. John A. Rae, Races, Fire Works, and a dance in the evening."

Theodore Roosevelt was not very successful as a cattle rancher. He was probably more concerned with his health and other matters, for he was independently wealthy. The terrible winter of 1886-1887 gave him a great setback, as it did most other ranchers of the area.

Roosevelt lived in North Dakota for two years and spent summers there during the next four years, and he never forgot his vigorous good times there. In 1898 he remembered the hard-riding ranchers and cowboys when he recruited his First U.S. Volunteer Cavalry for the war with Spain, and most of this crack outfit was made up of

Western men. He must have remembered the Rough Rider Hotel in Medora too, for he took this name for his cavalry—a name that has gone down in history—the Rough Riders.

In 1900, running for vice president under William McKinley, Roosevelt made a campaign visit to Medora and was enthusiastically greeted there. After McKinley was assassinated in 1901, a cowboy walked into Joe Ferris's store and reminded him of Ferris's prediction about Roosevelt becoming president. After seventeen years, the prediction had come true.

THE MARQUIS AND THE MEAT MADNESS

Another remarkable young man of pioneer-day Medora was a wealthy French aristocrat, the Marquis de Mores. He also had made a hunting trip in North Dakota and was so taken with the area's possibilities that he decided to build a packing plant where the cattle were being raised. De Mores thought this would eliminate many of the problems of getting meat from the hoof to the local butcher shop.

He planned to build his packing plant in Little Missouri, but when some arrangements fell through he bought land across the river and built his plant there. It opened in 1883. The town of Little Missouri withered and died. De Mores named the town that grew up around the packing plant Medora in honor of his wife, the former Medora Von Hoffman of New York.

The marquis's neighbors did not think too highly of him. They resented his special car on the railroad, and when he began to fence his land, real trouble broke out. During one squabble, a man was killed. De Mores was tried for murder and acquitted.

De Mores's wife, the marquise, was a beautiful red-haired young woman, for whom the marquis built a twenty-eight room chateau overlooking the Little Missouri River. Staffed with many servants, the mansion was a unique social center on the frontier, where many local people and prominent visitors from the East and abroad were entertained. Most of them came for the hunting. Theodore

The twenty-eight room Château de Mores, overlooking the Missouri River, was built by the Marquis de Mores for his wife, a beautiful redhead.

Roosevelt was sometimes a vistor, but he and the marquis were both too strong-willed to get along very well together.

On September 4, 1885, the *Bismarck Tribune's* headline read: "She Killed Three Bears," followed by the story "The Marquise, wife of Marquis de Mores, has returned from her hunt in the Rocky Mountains, where she killed two cinnamon bears and one large grizzly bear. The accomplished lady, who was a few years ago one of New York City's popular society belles, is now the queen of the Rocky Mountains and the champion huntress of the great northwest."

Lacking any success in his many businesses in the region, the marquis and his wife suddenly departed. Their château remained as it was for almost fifty years, until it was taken over by the State Historical Society in 1936. After leaving North Dakota, the marquis went hunting in Africa. There he was ambushed and killed by his native guides at the age of thirty-eight. The marquise was injured while serving as a nurse in World War I and died of her injuries in 1920.

CREATIVE AND INGENIOUS PEOPLE

Norwegian sculptor Paul Fjelde, a student of Lorado Taft, is one of the most prominent artists associated with North Dakota. Fjelde was commissioned by the state of North Dakota to do a bust of Abraham Lincoln that was presented to Norway in 1914. Jacob Fjelde, also a prominent North Dakota sculptor, is best known for his statues of Norwegian writer Henrik Ibsen. His bust of Ibsen at Wahpeton was given to the people of Richland County by the Norwegian people of the county on Norwegian Independence Day in 1912.

When the first steamboat chugged up the Yellowstone River, artist George Catlin was aboard. He spent much time in North Dakota studying and painting the Indians and other Western subjects for which he gained a great reputation. He also was well known as a writer on Western subjects.

Other visiting artists were John James Audubon, who painted many of the birds of North Dakota, and Swiss artist Carl Bodmer.

A contemporary artist of Western subjects is rancher Einar Olstad. His paintings are devoted almost entirely to activities of cattle ranching, cowboys, and other Western scenes. As a blacksmith and ironworker, he fashioned among other creations the wrought iron plaques of Theodore Roosevelt on a bucking bronco that decorate the gates of the Theodore Roosevelt National Memorial Park.

Painter and taxidermist J.D. Allen of Mandan was known for his handsome mountings of many of the animals shot by Theodore Roosevelt, as well as the trophies of visiting royalty.

Among authors associated with North Dakota, one of the best remembered is Maxwell Anderson, who lived in Jamestown and went to school there. He won the Pulitzer Prize for drama in 1933 for *Both Your Houses.*

A North Dakota poet of wide reputation is James W. Foley, who worked on the staff of the *Bismarck Tribune*. His best-known works are *Prairie Breezes* and *Voices of Song.*

Much of the writing of North Dakota has come from the pioneer experience. Some settlers gained fame in writing about the early times. One of these was Linda Slaughter. She came to Dakota Territory with her husband. She buried her first-born son on the lonely prairie. She heard the whistling arrows of attacking Indians. Her life as a postmistress at Bismarck and many other experiences of frontier days found their way into her writing. Her work was especially popular in eastern newspapers and it provides some of the best research material on life in those days.

Another pioneer writer was Joseph Henry Taylor, who lived a full life as a hunter, trapper, and author. As postmaster of Washburn, his first post office was a hole chopped into a tree. Taylor wrote his stories as he set them in type by hand, printing and publishing all of them himself. Among his books are *Kaleidoscopic Lives* and *Frontier and Indian Lives.*

In the field of the performing arts, probably the best-known North Dakota man of modern days has been popular television musician, band leader, and showman Lawrence Welk. Another popular musician from North Dakota is singer Peggy Lee. Actress Angie Dickinson came from Kulm. Renowned cowboy star Tom Mix lived for a while at Medora, where he married Olive M. Stokes. At the time they were both circus performers.

Retired television newsman Eric Sevareid and baseball star Roger Maris, who hit a record-breaking sixty-one home runs in a season, are other well-known North Dakota persons.

Among the most productive scientists of the state are Dr. Henry L. Bolley and Dr. Lawrence R. Waldron, both of North Dakota State University. Waldron probably has contributed more to the North Dakota economy than any other person. When wheat rust threatened to destroy the state's valuable wheat crops, Dr. Waldron developed wheats that would resist the rust, resulting in multimillion dollar savings each year.

Another important North Dakota crop is flax. When it was threatened with destruction by a deadly wilt, Bolley produced a type of flax that would resist the wilt.

In the field of medicine, Konrad Elias Birkbough was the discoverer of a cure for erysipelas, a skin disease.

One of the inventions most used by people today is credited to

D.H. Houston, who developed and patented the roll film type of camera. Industrialist George Eastman bought his patent and made the Kodak camera known throughout the world. There are some who say that Houston called his camera a Kodak, a variation in spelling of his state's name, in honor of North Dakota. Houston also developed a type of wheat that produced a much larger yield and patented an improved type of disc plow.

SUCH INTERESTING PEOPLE

Renowned explorer Vilhjalmur Stefansson attended the University of North Dakota and was always getting into scrapes. He went to very few classes and the story is told that he went to only the first day of his calculus class. The professor permitted him to take the final examination, on which he received a grade of 98 percent. The professor said that he had done quite well for having come to class only one day, but Stefansson shot back, "If I had not come here that first day I'd have gotten one hundred."

Another pioneer traveler was Colonel Carl Ben Eielson, born at Hatton. After he served in World War I, his hometown friends bought him a plane in which he barnstormed in North Dakota. He then went to Alaska where he was one of the early aviation leaders, flying the territory's first airmail. In 1928 he made a flight over the Arctic from Point Barrow to Sptizbergen with noted explorer Sir Hubert Wilkins. They also flew numerous flights in Antarctica. Eielson was killed in a rescue flight in Siberia.

In the field of public life, one of North Dakota's best-known members of the United States Senate was Gerald P. Nye of Cooperstown. Senator A.J. Gronna was one of six senators who voted against the United States' entrance into World War I.

A local politician, Bud Reeves of Buxton, was one of the first persons to use a house trailer. He had a log cabin built on a wagon and traveled across the state, ringing a bell to announce his speeches. Before speaking he always unfurled the American flag and brought out his live captive eagle.

W.D. Boyce of Lisbon gained prominence by being the first to introduce the idea of the Boy Scout movement into the United States. Another innovator was N.P. Lindberg, a Rugby florist. At a national convention of florists, Lindberg made a speech in which he said, "In North Dakota, we say it with flowers." The phrase "say it with flowers" was selected as the slogan of the florists' group and became popular throughout the nation.

Prominent North Dakota religious leaders include Father Jerome Hunt, who for forty years was a missionary at St. Michael's Mission near Fort Totten. Among his accomplishments was the publishing of books in the Sioux language. Father George Antoine Belcourt was one of the most noted missionaries to the Indians; he helped found the community of Belcourt, named in his honor. Father J.B. Genin was influential in arranging the Treaty of Fort Abercrombie between the Sioux and Chippewa, which gave eastern North Dakota relative peace from Indian attack during the troubled 1870s.

A popular clergyman of a later period was the Reverend Robert Wainwright, once a missionary in Labrador. He raised funds for his church work by lecturing dressed in Labrador costume and demonstrating the use of a forty-foot (twelve-meter) bull whip He could flick water from a glass with the tip of the whip without upsetting the glass.

Among Indians prominent in the state's history, Running Antelope's appearance was known throughout the country. His likeness was used on the old large-sized five-dollar bill.

One of the best-known men in the region was Grant Marsh, who served an incredible sixty years as a steamboat captain. Captain Marsh brought back word of the Custer massacre and carried the wounded to Bismarck in his boat.

A young North Dakota heroine was sixteen-year-old Hazel Miner of Center. She and her younger sister and brother became lost in one of North Dakota's fierce blizzards. Searchers found her frozen body the next morning, covering her brother and sister and holding down the blanket that kept them from freezing. She had sacrificed her life for them. A statue stands in the town of Center, as a memorial to her heroic act.

Teaching and Learning

Higher educational institutions in North Dakota are two state universities and branches, four state colleges, and two private colleges.

The first institution of higher education in North Dakota was Jamestown College, founded by Presbyterians in 1883.

A few months after Jamestown College was founded, the territorial legislature voted funds for a university. Old Main, the first building, was begun at Grand Forks that year, and the university started operations on September 8, 1884. The University of North Dakota was one of the few public universities in the country to open before its territory had become a state. Among its interesting academic accomplishments is its record as the second institution in the nation to provide courses in radio. The University of North Dakota today enrolls nearly nine thousand students.

North Dakota State University at Fargo was founded in 1889 as the North Dakota Agricultural College. When the cornerstone of the administration building was laid, the elaborate ceremonies had begun before it was discovered there was no flag for the ceremony. An ingenious student improvised one from a pair of overalls, and the day was saved. Federal grants of land to the state university totaled 130,000 acres (52,600 hectares), providing a substantial endowment. Experiment stations at Fargo and Williston offer "the most efficient system of research I have ever observed," according to former Montana Senator Leo Borah. Present enrollment is nearly eight thousand students.

The educational institutions of North Dakota underwent one of the strangest financial experiences in American history in 1895 when Governor Roger Allin vetoed most appropriations for all the state colleges and universities. The schools managed to keep open only through the generosity of public subscribers and the faculty's willingness to serve without pay for a period. Finally the funds were restored.

North Dakota state colleges are at Dickinson, Mayville, Minot, and Valley City.

In addition to Jamestown College, the only private college is Mary College for women at Bismarck.

The first school in North Dakota was opened at the original Pembina settlement and continued until the settlers moved from Pembina in 1823. As settlements expanded, schools were opened, many of them taught by mothers or by itinerant teachers. The first teacher at Fargo was a fifteen-year-old girl, Mary Nelson. However, the settlers were determined to have their children educated, and that determination is shown by the remarkable fact that between 1853 and statehood in 1889, 1,362 schools had been opened in North Dakota.

When statehood came, North Dakota had a well-organized public school system, perhaps the best ever achieved by any state at the time of its statehood. As in other states, federal and state lands were given for school use. In many states these were squandered by poor management or fraud, but it is said that school lands have been better guarded in North Dakota than in most of the other states. At the urging of territorial superintendent W.H.H. Beadle, the state constitution prohibited the selling of school lands at less than $10 per acre and provided that western land titles would always be held by the schools.

One of the finest specialized schools in the state is the State School for the Deaf at Devils Lake. The teaching methods and other practices have made the school a model for study by similar institutions all over the world. The State School for the Blind is located at Grand Forks.

Two different plans for teaching industrial subjects were originated in North Dakota. These were the so-called North Dakota plan and the Babcock plan, developed by E.J. Babcock of the University of North Dakota School of Mines. The State Normal and Industrial School at Ellendale gave the first free course in manual training ever offered in the United States.

One of the country's more unusual educational institutions is the Summer School of Fine Arts at the International Peace Gardens, where music, art, and dance are taught. There is also a track and field training camp held at the Peace Gardens each year in August.

Enchantment of North Dakota

BISMARCK

While standing in a waving wheat field, one symbol of North Dakota of both past and present, a visitor may gaze in admiration at a symbol of modern North Dakota—the surprising skyscraper capitol, towering nineteen stories above the wheat fields that come almost to its door.

This prairie skyscraper was built during the depth of the Great Depression and finished in 1932. Many argued that to build a skyscraper designed to save land in a city where land stretched almost endlessly in all directions made little sense, but one result of this striking design was economy of construction. For $2 million the people of the state received a building that would cost many times that today. In addition, it is considered one of the most efficient government buildings anywhere. As one school of architecture points out, "The new style in capitols seems to follow the lead of Nebraska, Louisiana, and North Dakota."

North Dakota's state capitol building is a skyscraper.

The most striking exterior feature is the assembly of bronze statues created by sculptor Edgar Miller of Chicago—including statues of Indian, Hunter, Trapper, Farmer, Miner, and a figure symbolic of the mothers of North Dakota.

The capitol interior is truly distinctive. Memorial Hall, 342 feet (104 meters) long and 42 feet (13 meters) high, is lined with soaring fluted bronze columns. The windows provide a striking view of the city and the winding Missouri River. The interior decoration of rare woods, beautiful stone, and handsome metal work is especially beautiful.

A fascinating sight on the capitol grounds is the log cabin of Theodore Roosevelt's Chimney Butte ranch, moved to its present location and dedicated as a memorial to the rancher-president.

The State Historical Society Museum, housed in Liberty Memorial Building, displays Indian and pioneer relics. The well-known statue *Pioneer Family* by Avard Fairbanks stands in the grounds, as does the statue of Sacajawea, the Indian woman guide of Lewis and Clark.

Another display of early Bismarck is offered in the Camp Hancock Museum, on the site of the encampment around which the city sprang. The location of Bismarck was known as one of the best fords on the entire Missouri River. Bismarck's earliest importance was as a steamboat port. When the railroad arrived, Bismarck gained new prominence and the modern city was born. The date of settlement is usually given as 1873.

During the early period, much of the town's life revolved around Fort Abraham Lincoln, across the river. The early fort has been restored as Fort Abraham Lincoln State Park. One park attraction is the reconstruction of Old Slant Village, a town site of the Mandan Indians. Here may be seen the typical earth lodge construction of the Mandan. The old blockhouse and other fort buildings from which George Armstrong Custer departed toward his last stand also have been restored.

Bismarck was named to honor the Iron Chancellor of Germany, Otto Furst von Bismarck. The hope was that this honor would persuade Germany to provide capital for development of the city. The days are gone when a party in Bismarck might provide refreshments of champagne and buffalo tongue and when "men died in only two ways, getting shot or drinking too much." The frontier city of only a generation or two ago has become the progressive capital of a modern state.

The city of Mandan, across the river from Bismarck, commemorates the villages of the Mandan who once occupied much of the region. The present city is an oil refining center.

FARGO

North Dakota's largest city, Fargo had its start in 1871 during the railroad boom.

It soon became a Red River port and the distributing point for a vast area. The modern city is still a leading transportation and distribution center. The importance of the city in this regard is not reflected accurately by its population. As headquarters of a vast agricultural empire, Fargo does the business of many cities ten or twelve times its size in population.

The city's growing industry now boasts more than a hundred manufacturing firms, a contrast to the two harness and horse collar factories of Fargo in 1901.

Fargo was named in honor of William C. Fargo, one of the founders of the Wells Fargo Company. Fargo was also a director of the Northern Pacific Railroad, a chief contributor to the city's economic vitality.

The first Christmas celebration in Fargo was quite interesting. A Christmas tree had been set up and then stolen. The residents of nearby Moorhead, Minnesota, were suspected, and they were hanged in effigy. The tree returned as mysteriously as it had disappeared. Decorated with silver half-dollars, it was set up in front of what is now 27 Front Street. A locomotive headlight was used to illuminate the tree, and each child in the community was given one of the half-dollars as a commemoration of the event.

An English writer gave a fascinating description of Fargo in 1879:

"In Fargo, built of stone and brick, there are already three good hotels, and another in contemplation; rather too many drinking saloons; a concert and ball room, where recently a grand subscription ball was given for which gentlemen's tickets were stated to be $25. There is a courthouse and two portly courteous judges.... An Opera-Comique is in successful operation.... The immense and varied collections of agricultural implements are strikingly indicative of the breaking in of new lands."

Horse-drawn streetcars began operating in 1879, but when the ground thawed in spring 1880 the tracks vanished into the mud.

Fargo suffered its most disastrous fire in 1893, with a loss of nearly $5 million, but the city quickly rebuilt. The flood of 1897 was one of the worst disasters in the city's history.

For a few years, Fargo had a reputation as a divorce center. Many wealthy and prominent persons took up temporary residence in Fargo in the 1890s to take advantage of the ninety-day divorce law then in effect.

An opera house was built in 1893, and the city has long attracted theater companies and prominent theatrical personalities. Fargo's Little Country Theatre was one of the pioneer efforts in the nation's community theater history.

In 1959 Fargo was chosen as an All-American City. One point of interest is the Forsberg House, displaying an exhibit of Americana. At Oak Grove Park the Red River takes such a sharp bend that visitors look west across the river to Minnesota, instead of east as would be expected.

Probably the most notable structure in North Dakota, at least the one most famous around the world, is the incredible television tower of station KTHI-TV, located about midway between Fargo and Grand Forks. Soaring to an unbelievable height of 2,063 feet (629 meters) it is the second tallest structure in the world. A building this high could contain 230 stories. It provides television reception for a vast area of North Dakota and Minnesota.

Opposite: Two views of Fargo—looking west at the skyline (top) and an aerial view looking north (bottom).

OTHER CITIES

Grand Forks takes its name from the forks formed by the the joining of the Red and Red Lake rivers. It has close ties with East Grand Forks, on the Minnesota side of the Red. The two communities are joined by John F. Kennedy Memorial Bridge.

A Grand Forks pioneer was Captain Alexander Griggs, who freighted goods on the Red River in flatboats. His competition was furnished by George Winship. Once both Winship and Griggs loaded flatboat fleets with cargos for Pembina and Winnipeg. Winship got away first, but Griggs and his crew vowed to catch up. In a shallow part of the river Winship had to transfer his cargos to lighter craft, and Griggs's team caught up. However, several casks of beer were lost from Winship's cargo; they were retrieved by Griggs's crew, who drank the contents with gusto.

The Griggs crew became so incapacitated with drink that before the men could proceed, the river froze, and they had to build temporary huts. The crew spent the winter where Grand Forks now stands—the first known residents of the site.

When spring came, Griggs continued on with his cargo, but later came back and built a squatter's cabin at the Red Lake River's mouth. In 1871 he built the settlement's first frame residence. A post office was established a year later, and the city was on its way.

Attractions in Grand Forks include its symphony orchestra and the University of North Dakota. The Eternal Flame of Knowledge, a sphere of steel girders weighing half a ton (more than 450 kilograms), dedicated to the memory of past presidents of the university, stands on the campus. The Oriental Room of the university's Chester Fritz Library has a display of Oriental tapestries and other art items.

Turtle River State Park and Grand Forks Air Force Base (occupied by seventeen thousand people) are both in the vicinity.

The Minuteman II missile unit at Grand Forks, equipped with 150 missiles located in buried, hardened concrete launchers stretching across most of North Dakota, was considered one of the important units in the United States defense.

Buffalo Monument, Jamestown.

Jamestown is identified by its landmark, "the world's largest buffalo," a sixty-ton (fifty-four metric-ton) statue of that majestic animal towering to a height of twenty feet (six meters). Nearby is an authentic prairie school, restored as nearly as possible to conditions of fifty years ago, with books of the period, desks, and other items.

Near the city are Arrowwood Wildlife Refuge, Jamestown Dam and Recreation Area, and Whitestone Battlefield State Park, the site of the most savage battle with the Indians in the state's history. The park also features a museum of Indian items.

It has been said that Minot "sprang up overnight with the arrival of the Great Northern Railroad in 1887." The city takes its name from Henry D. Minot, a capitalist in the East and a classmate of

Theodore Roosevelt. Some aged residents can still remember when the industry of buffalo bone collecting provided a living for many who gathered the bones on the prairie and brought them to Minot's bone piles, where they were bought for fertilizer and other uses.

Some may still remember the first Christmas tree. Since there were no churches, the Christmas tree was decorated and placed in the Jack Doyle saloon, at the corner where Main and Central meet today.

Today's Minot is a center of the lignite industry.

Minot's Theodore Roosevelt Park provides a fine twenty-eight-acre (eleven-hectare) zoo; there are ten acres (four hectares) landscaped in formal gardens and lawns, concerts in the band shell, and other attractions. The statue of Roosevelt as a Rough Rider, presented to the city by Dr. Henry Waldo Coe, a long-time friend of Roosevelt, is a prominent feature of the park. It was dedicated to the schoolchildren of the region, whose pennies purchased the statue's base.

There is an Air Force base near Minot.

Williston has long been a leading grain market. During the cruel drought and depression years of the 1930s, however, the city suffered. Today Williston is still a leading grain center and cattle market, but many additional activities have made it a thriving and bustling communtity of great potential. Garrison Lake now assures water for the area. A constant flow of new industries has added to the stability of the growing city.

Handsomely landscaped Spring Lake Park, with its interesting zoo, is a scenic attraction. Another is the Scenic Drive from Williston to New Town, through the Garrison Reservoir northern area. Oil wells, Badlands, and the lake shores are all notable sights. Bears Bridge is an engineering landmark.

Fort Buford State Historical Park is seventeen miles (twenty-seven kilometers) from Williston. The regimental headquarters building of the old fort is still standing, and the old stone powder house may also be seen. Here are memories of the surrender of Sitting Bull at the fort in 1881, which brought an end to the Indian disturbances.

OTHER POINTS OF INTEREST

The principal tourist attraction of North Dakota is the 70,374 scenic acres (28,479 hectares) of Theodore Roosevelt National Memorial Park. The three sections of the park—North Unit, South Unit, and Elkhorn Ranch Unit, all on the Little Missouri River—preserve the scenic Badlands region much as it was when Theodore Roosevelt lived in the area.

Roosevelt would have approved of the conservation measure that brought a small buffalo herd to the region, restoring a part of the wildlife that was once so abundant. Antelope and deer are still numerous, and several large prairie dog towns are among the few in the country that still survive. Eagles, hawks, falcons, and smaller birds abound in the region.

The people of North Dakota are proud of this, the only National Memorial Park yet established in the United States where memories of a great man combine so properly with scenic beauty. The Badlands are "grand, dismal and majestic," as General Alfred H. Sully described them. Water and wind have sculpted a fantastic expanse of canyons, buttes, tablelands, and twisted hills. Here and there fumes ascend from lignite ignited by lightning, around which the multicolored clinkers known as scoria have banked the eternal fires.

Roosevelt himself once wrote about the park: "I grow very fond of this place.... [it] has a desolate, grim beauty, that has a curious fascination for me." A host of travelers have responded to that fascination since that day.

Historic Medora is the gateway to the southern section of the Roosevelt Memorial. The city is a kind of living museum of two of the most unlikely characters to be found on a frontier—Roosevelt and the French aristocrat, the Marquis de Mores. The Château de Mores State Monument preserves the ruins of the marquis's ill-fated packing plant. His huge château, now a museum, retains all the relics he and his wife left when they hurried away and never returned.

The town of Medora is being restored as much as possible to its original condition. Tourists may still see the Rough Rider Hotel,

built by the marquis, which gave the Roosevelt Rough Riders their famous name.

Another outstanding park of an entirely different nature from Roosevelt is the International Peace Gardens, nestled in the beautiful Turtle Mountains on the border of North Dakota and Manitoba, Canada. The diverse natural beauty of the terrain has been combined with splendid formal gardens and displays.

The idea for such a garden was conceived by Henry J. Moore and adopted by the National Association of Gardeners of America. The site was selected for its natural beauty and because it is about halfway from the east and west ends of the great undefended border between the United States and Canada. The state of North Dakota and the province of Manitoba donated the land, and fifty thousand people from all over North America assembled for the dedication on July 14, 1932. A cairn of native stone was unveiled during the ceremonies, bearing the inscription "To God in His glory, We two nations dedicate this garden and pledge ourselves that as long as men shall live, we will not take up arms against one another."

Each year the park is rededicated in honor of the more than 150 years of peace along one of the world's longest borders.

The Verendrye National Monument near Stanley commemorates the first European visitors to North Dakota. Another commemorative site is Fort Dilts State Park, near Rhame. Here eighty wagons of a Montana-bound immigrant train, under Indian attack, were gathered in a circular defense formation for fourteen days. The park is named for Jefferson Dilts, who was killed during the engagement. When the wagon train moved on, the immigrants left a box of poisoned hardtack, which killed many Indians.

Fort Abercrombie, another state park, marks the pioneer outpost once known as the Gateway to the Dakotas. Blockhouses, guardhouses, stockades, and cabins of the first military post in North Dakota have been restored.

Another outpost, Fort Totten, near the town of Devils Lake, is now a state monument. It was the last stop for travelers before 300 miles (480 kilometers) of wilderness. Today it is the only fort of its type still in existence, with nineteen original buildings standing.

Devils Lake has long been a popular resort of the region. At one time, the Chautauqua of Creel's Bay was the third largest entertainment center of its kind in the country. The lake is said to be the home of a sea monster and phantom ships. St. Michael's Indian Mission, a monument to Father Jerome Hunt, has a display of pioneer cabins and other materials. Sullys Hill National Game Preserve is fourteen miles (twenty-two kilometers) from the town of Devils Lake, and Skyline Drive provides an exceptionally picturesque view along the Devils Lake shore.

Fort Mandan Historic Site recalls the winter spent in the region by Lewis and Clark on their way up the Missouri. The original buildings were burned by the Sioux in 1805. The changing of the river channel has made it impossible to locate the exact site, but the area recognized at present is in the immediate region.

Nearby is another site of interest—mammoth Garrison Dam—210 feet (64 meters) high, 12,000 feet (3,658 meters) long, requiring 66,459,068 cubic yards (50,811,612 cubic meters) of material to complete. The town of Riverdale is an ultramodern center, developed for the construction of the dam.

Garrison Dam powerhouse.

Garrison Dam Spillway.

Farther down the river, near Fort Yates in the Standing Rock Indian Reservation, is the grave of Sitting Bull, one of America's best-known Indian leaders.

Many persons throughout the country help support an unusual institution near Beach. Father Cassedy's Home on the Range for Boys provides homeless and needy boys a home. The youths help maintain a 1,900-acre (769-hectare) working ranch.

Portal is a leading port of entry on the Canadian border. One of the world's unusual golf courses is its international golf course, with parts of the course in each country. It is remembered for its international hole-in-one, which was shot from the eighth-hole tee in Canada to the cup in the United States.

Rugby has an unusual attraction. Only a half mile (.8 kilometer) from the town is the Geographic Center of North America, located by the United States Geological Survey. The site is marked by a monument.

Grafton, a thriving community, is the stopping point for visitors to North Dakota's first community, Pembina, which took the Indian name for the red highbush cranberry. Pembina State Monument and Museum preserves relics of the pioneers.

From pioneer hardships to the rich abundance of modern farms, mines, and factories in little more than a lifetime is the capsule history of North Dakota.

Handy Reference Section

Instant Facts

Became the 39th or 40th state, November 2, 1889
Capital—Bismarck, settled 1873
Nickname—Sioux State or Flickertail State
State motto—"Liberty and Union, Now and Forever, One and Inseparable"
State bird—Western meadowlark
State fish—Northern pike
State tree—American elm *(ulmus Americana)*
State flower—Wild prairie rose *(rose blanda* or *arkansana)*
State stone—Teredo petrified wood
State song—"North Dakota Hymn"
Area—70,665 square miles (183,022 square kilometers)
Rank in area—17th
Greatest length (north to south)—210 miles (338 kilometers)
Greatest width (east to west)—360 miles (579 kilometers)
Geographic center—5 miles (8 kilometers) southwest of McClusky
Highest point—3,506 feet (1,069 meters), White Butte, Slope County
Lowest point—750 feet (229 meters), on the Red River
Mean elevation—1,900 feet (579 meters)
Number of counties—53
Population—600,000 (1980 projection)
Rank in population—45th
Population density—8.4 per square mile (3.2 per square kilometer), 1980 projection
Rank in density—44th
Population center—In Wells County, 13.5 miles (21.7 kilometers) southeast of Fessenden
Illiteracy rate—.8%
Birthrate—15.2 per 1,000
Infant mortality rate—17 per 1,000 births
Physicians per 100,000—103
Principal cities—Fargo   55,815   (1970 census)
                 Grand Forks   42,581
                 Bismarck   38,123
                 Minot   32,823
                 Jamestown   15,078
                 Dickinson   12,496
                 Minot Base   12,077
                 Williston   11,280

Opposite: **Pioneer Family** *sculpture at Bismarck.*

You Have a Date with History

1682—La Salle claims for France the area drained by Missouri River
1738—Sieur de La Vérendrye is first European visitor
1742—Vérendrye's sons pay another visit
1762—France transfers claims to Spain
1763—England given portions drained by northerly flowing rivers
1768—Jonathan Carver explores
1797—David Thompson explores, maps; Chaboillez establishes first trading post at Pembina
1801—Alexander Henry, Jr., establishes post at Pembina
1803—Louisiana Purchase; land drained by Missouri River becomes United States territory
1804—Lewis and Clark winter in North Dakota
1812—Selkirk colonists make first settlement
1823—Stephen H. Long establishes Canadian boundary
1829—Fort Union established by American Fur Company
1831—Fort Clark established
1837—Smallpox epidemic strikes Indians
1848—Father George Belcourt opens missions
1857—Fort Abercrombie established
1860—Upper Missouri River gets regular steamboat runs
1861—Dakota Territory organized
1866—Fort Buford started
1871—Railroad reaches Fargo
1873—Fort Abraham Lincoln established; railroad reaches Bismarck
1875—Bonanza farms begin operation
1876—Custer's massacre announcement comes from Bismarck
1883—Bismarck becomes territorial capital
1887—One of worst winters in history
1889—Statehood
1897—Flood causes heavy damage in Red River Valley
1909—First law in state concerning child labor
1916—Nonpartisan League elects first governor
1917—World War I begins; 31,269 from North Dakota see service
1919—Bank of North Dakota established
1921—First state governor in United States history "recalled"
1929—Terrible drought begins
1930—Fire destroys state capitol
1941—World War II begins; 60,016 are in service; 1,939 lose their lives
1947—Theodore Roosevelt National Memorial Park authorized
1951—Oil discovered near Tioga
1953—President Eisenhower speaks at "closure" of Garrison Dam
1957—North Dakota creates Economic Development Commission
1958—Potato flake plant established at Grand Forks
1960—First salt mining

1965—First sugar beet refinery at Drayton
1966—Stanton pioneers in lignite-fired generation of electricity
1967—First "unit train" to haul lignite put on line serving Beulah, Stanton, and Mandan
1968—Garrison Diversion Project increases state's water supply
1973—Omega All-Weather Navigation System completed
1975—Legislature ratifies ERA amendment

Thinkers, Doers, Fighters

People of renown who have been associated with North Dakota

Anderson, Maxwell
Birkbough, Konrad Elias
Bolley, Henry L.
Catlin, George
Eielson, Carl Ben
Fjelde, Jacob
Fjelde, Paul
Foley, James W.
Houslon, D.H.
Maris, Roger
Mores, Marquis de
Mores, Marquise de
Nye, Gerald P.
Olstad, Einar
Roosevelt, Theodore
Sevareid, Eric
Slaughter, Linda
Stefansson, Vilhjalmur
Taylor, Joseph Henry
Waldron, Lawrence R.

Governors of the State of North Dakota

John Miller 1889-1891
Andrew Burke 1891-1893
Eli Shortridge 1893-1895
Roger Allin 1895-1897
Frank Briggs 1897-1898
Joseph M. Devine 1898-1899
Fred B. Fancher 1899-1901
Frank White 1901-1905
E.Y. Sarles 1905-1907
John Burke 1907-1913
L.B. Hanna 1913-1917
Lynn J. Frazier 1917-1921
R.A. Nestos 1921-1925
Arthur G. Sorlie 1925-1928
Walter Maddock 1928-1929
George F. Schafer 1929-1933
William Langer 1933-1934
Ole Olson 1934-1935
Thomas H. Moodie 1935
Walter Welford 1935-1937
William Langer 1937-1939
John Moses 1939-1945
Fred Aandahl 1945-1951
Norman Brunsdale 1951-1957
John E. Davis 1957-1961
William L. Guy 1961-1973
Arthur A. Link 1973-

*Right: A deer near Garrison Dam.
Below: The International Peace Gardens near Dunseith.*

Index

page numbers in bold type indicate illustrations

Absaroke Indians, 22
Agates, 47
Agricultural tribes, 22, 23, 36
Agriculture, 53, **53**, 54
Air Force bases, 78, 80
Alfalfa, 55
Algonquin Indians, 22
All-American City, 77
Allen, J.D., 67
Allin, Roger, 71
Altamont Moraine, 11
American Fur Company, 35
Anderson, Maxwell, 67
Animals, 48-51
Anson Northrup (steamboat), 60
Area, state, 87
Arikara Indians, 22, 28, 31
Arrowwood Lake, 15, 51
Arrowwood Wildlife Refuge, 51, 79
Artists, 67
Assiniboine River, Canada, 12
Assiniboin Indians, 22
Astor, John Jacob, 65
Audubon, John James, 67
Authors, 67, 68
Babcock, E.J., 72
Babcock plan, 72
Badlands of North Dakota, 15, 16, **17**, 19, 47, 80, 81
Bank of North Dakota, 44, 57
Barley, 54
Barnard, Alonzo, 46
Beach (town), 85
Beadle, W.H.H., 72
Bear, grizzly, 50
Bears Bridge, 80
Beaver River, 13
Belcourt, George Antoine, 46, 70
Belcourt (town), 70
Belmont, 60
Benton, Jessie, 35
Benton, Thomas Hart, 35
Bentonite clay, 57
Berthold, Bartholomew, 36
Biddle (of Lewis & Clark party), 31
Big Bellies (Indians), 22, 33
Big Canoe (hollow log), 23
Big Horn River, Montana, 9, 10
Big Mound, Battle of, 35
Bird, state, 87
Birds, 51, 81
Birkbough, Konrad Elias, 68

Bismarck, Otto Furst von, 74
Bismarck (city), 9, 10, 21, 22, 31, 38, 41, 42, 46, 57, 60, 61, 68, 70, 73-75, 87
Bismarck Tribune, 10, 61, 66, 67
Black-billed cuckoo, 51
Black Hills, SD, 38, 60
Blacks, 46
Blind, State School for, 72
Bodmer, Carl, 67
Bois de Sioux River, 12
Bolley, Henry L., 68
Bonanza farms, 39, 43, 53
Borah, Leo, 71
Border, North Dakota-Canada, 11, 30, 83
Both Your Houses, 67
Bottineau, 40, 52
Boulder rings, 21
Bowman, 57
Boyce, W.D., 70
Boy Scouts, 70
Bridges, 78, 80
Briquettes, lignite, 57
British in North Dakota, 30
Buffalo (animal), 23, **24**, 48, 49, **49**, 51, 80, 81
Buffalo (town), 18
Buffalo dance, Indian, **24**, 27
Buffalo Monument, Jamestown, 79, **79**
Buffalo parks, 23
Bull boats, Indian, 26
Burial customs, Indians, 25, 26
Burke, John (Honest John), 43
Burlington, 45
Burrowing owl, 51
Business enterprises, state-run, 43, 44, 57
Buxton, 69
Caddoan Indians, 22
Camp Hancock Museum, Bismarck, 74
Canada, 11, 12, 18, 29, 35, 39, 83, 85
Canadian people, 46
Cannonball River, 13, 28
Capital, state, 73
Capitals, territorial, 36, 41
Capitols, state, 42, 44, 73, **73**, 74
"Caprock" erosion, **17**
Casey, Lyman, 42
Cassedy, Father, 85
Casualties, war, 43, 45
Catholic church, 46
Catlin, George, 24, 27, 67

Cattle, 54
Center (town), 70
Chaboillez, Charles, 30
Charbonneau, Pompey, 34
Charbonneau, Toussaint, 34
Chase, Stuart, 53
Château de Mores, 65, 66, **66**, 81
Château de Mores State Monument, 81
Chautauqua, 84
Chernozem (silty soil), 18
Chester Fritz Library, Grand Forks, 78
Cheyenne Indians, 22
Child labor law, 43
Chimney Butte ranch, 63, 74
Chippewa Indians, 22, 70
Chronology, 88, 89
Cities, principal, 87
Clark, William, 26, 30-34, 40, 50, 74, 84
Clays, 57
Climate, 20
Clinker (scoria), 47, 58, 81
Clothing, Indian, 25
Coal, 16, 19, 45, 47, **56**, 57, 80, 81
Coe, Henry Waldo, 80
Colleges, 71, 72
Columnar cedar trees, 52
Communication, 61
Congress, U.S., 42
Conservation, 51, 52, 81
Constitution, state, 42, 72
Continental climate, 20
Cooperstown, 69
Coteau du Missouri, 11, 54
County seats, 43
Coyotes, 50, **50**
Cradleboards, Indian, 28
Crafts, Indian, 26
Crawford, Lewis, 35
Cream of Wheat, 55
Creel's Bay, 84
Crops, 54
Crow Indians, 9
Crowley Flint Quarry State Park, 26
Currier and Ives, 37, 40
Custer, George Armstrong, 9, 10, 38, **39**, 70, 74
Custer, Mrs. George Armstrong, 9, 10, 38
Dakota, derivation of name, 11
Dakota sandstone, 16
Dakota song sparrow, 51
Dakota Territory, 36, 37, 41, 42, 68

91

Dalrymple, Oliver, 39
Dams, 14, 51, 79, 84, **84, 85**
Deadwood, SD, 61
Deaf, State School for, 72
Deer, 48, 51, **90**
Democratic Party, 43
Density of population, 87
Depressions, economic, 39, 43, 44
Des Lacs Lakes, 15
Des Lacs River, 13
De Smet, Pierre Jean, 38
Devils Lake (town), 72, 83, 84
Devils Lake (lake), 15, 18, 84
Dickinson, Angie, 68
Dickinson (city), 64, 71
Dickinson Press, 64
Dilts, Jefferson, 83
Disasters, 40, 41, 44, 77
Disease, 29, 35
Divide, 14
Division of Mines and Mining Experiments, 57
Divorce law, 77
Douglas, William (Earl of Selkirk), 35
Drake, 44
Drift Plains, 11
Drift Prairie, 11, 54
Droughts, 15, 40, 43, 44
Dumoulin, Joseph, 46
Dunseith, 90
Eagles, 25
East Grand Forks, MN, 78
Eastman, George, 69
Economic Development Commission, 45
Edge, William, 46
Education, 71, 72
Eielson, Carl Ben, 69
Elkhorn Ranch, 63, 64, 81
Elk River (Missouri River), 12
Ellendale, 36, 72
Elmer, Oscar H., 46
Equal Rights Amendment, 45
Erosion, **17**, 52
Eternal Flame of Knowledge, Grand Forks, 78
Ethnic groups, 45, 46
Exploration, 29-35
Fairbanks, Avard, 74
Fargo, William C., 75
Fargo (city), 18, 21, 42, 47, 60, 71, 72, 75, **76,** 77
Fargo Industrial Park, **55**
Farming, 53, **53,** 54
Far West (steamboat), 9, 10
Ferris, Joe, 63, 65
Finnish people, 45
Fires, 15, 16, 40, 41, 44, 77
First U.S. Volunteer Cavalry, 64

Fish, state, 87
Fish and fishing, 51
Fitch, George, 12
Fjelde, Jacob, 67
Fjelde, Paul, 67
Flax, 54, 68
Flickertails (gophers), 48
Flickertail State, 48
Flint quarries, 21, 26
Floods, 40, 77
Flower, state, 52, 87
Flowers, 52
Foley, James W., 9, 10, 67
Foreclosures, mortgage, 44
Forest River, 12
Forests, 52
Forsberg House, Fargo, 77
Fort Abercrombie, 36, 70, 83
Fort Abercrombie State Park, 83
Fort Abraham Lincoln, 9, 10, 38, 74
Fort Abraham Lincoln State Park, 26-27, 74
Fort Berthold, 36, 59
Fort Berthold Indian reservation, 46
Fort Buford, 37, 39, 80
Fort Buford State Historical Park, 80
Fort Dilts State Park, 83
Fort Mandan, 31, 33, 34
Fort Mandan Historic Site, 84
Fort Rice, 61
Fort Totten, 70, 83
Fort Totten Indian reservation, 46
Fort Union, 35, 37, 49, 61
Fort Yates, 85
Fossils, 19, 20
Frazier, Lynn J., 43, 44
Frazier, Robert, 30
Frémont, John C., 35
French in North Dakota, 29
Fritz, Chester, 78
Frog Point, 60
Frontier and Indian Lives, 68
Frontier Scout (newspaper), 61
Fuller's earth, 57
Fur trading, 30, 32, 35, 38
Garrison (town), 36
Garrison Dam, 14, 50, 51, 84, **84, 85**
Garrison Lake, 80
Garrison Reservoir, 80
Gems, 47
Genin, J.B., 70
Geographic center, North America, 11, 85
Geographic center, state, 87
Geography, 11
Geology, 16
German people, 46

Glaciers, 16, 18
Glauber's salts, 47
Gold rush, Black Hills, 38
Golf course, Portal, 85
Good Furred Robe, 28
Goose River, 12
Gophers, 48
Governor, territorial, 36
Governors, state, 42, 43, 44, 71, 89
Grafton, 85
Grand Forks, 44, 47, 55, 57, 71, 72, 77, 78
Grand Forks Air Force Base, 78
Grant, Ulysses S., 42
Great Northern Railroad, 79
Griggs, Alexander, 78
Grizzly bear, 50
Gronna, A. J., 69
Gros Ventres Indians, 22, 33
Grouse, 51
Gulf of Mexico, 14
Hall of Fame, Washington, D.C., 43
Harrison, Benjamin, 42
Hastings, 28
Hatton, 69
Hay, 54
Heart River, 13, 22
Hebron, 21
Herman Beach, 18
Hidatsa Indians, 12, 22
Highest point, state, 15, 87
Highways, 61
Holy Hill of the Mandan Indians, 28
Home on the Range for Boys, 85
Horse Head Lake, 15
Horses, 25
Houston, D.H., 69
Hudson Bay, 14, 16
Hudson's Bay Company, 30, 35
Hunt, Jerome, 70, 84
Hunting, 49-51
Ibsen, Henrik, 67
Ice ages, 16
Iceland, people from, 45
Indians, 9, 12, 15, 16, 22-28, **24, 27,** 29, 30, 31, 32 33, 34, 35, 36, 37, 38, 39, 46, 49, 58, **59,** 70, 74, 79, 83, 85
Industrial education, 72
Industry, 54-57
Initiation ceremony, Mandan Indians, 27, **27**
International Peace Gardens, 72, 83, **90**
Inventors, 68-69
Inyan Bosdata (standing rock), 28

Irrigation, 45, 54
Jack Doyle saloon, Minot, 80
James River, 13, 14, 60
Jamestown, 41, 42, 67, 79
Jamestown College, 71
Jamestown Dam and Recreation Area, 79
Jayne, William, 36
Jim Lake, 15
Keepa, feast of, 27
Kellogg, Mark, 10
Kennedy, John F., Memorial Bridge, 78
Killdeer (town), 15
Killdeer Mountain, Battle of, 36
Killdeer Mountains, 15
Knife River, 13, 21
Kodak camera, 69
KTHI-TV television station, 77
Lake Agassiz (prehistoric), 18, 47
Lake Ashtabula, 15
Lake Dakota (prehistoric), 18
Lake Darling, 15
Lake Jessie, 35
Lake Manitoba, Canada, 18
Lake Oahe, 14
Lake of the Woods, Minnesota, 18
Lakes, 14, 15, 18
Lake Sakakawea, 14, 50
Lake Souris (prehistoric), 18
Lake Tschida, 15
Lake Upsilon, 15
Lake Winnipeg, Canada, 18
Lake Winnipegosis, Canada, 18
LaMoure, 41, 45
Langer, William, 44
Laramie, WY, 38
Lee, Peggy, 68
Legislature, state, 42, 45
Length, greatest, state, 87
Lewis, Meriwether, 30-34, **32,** 40, 47, 50, 74, 84
Liberty Memorial Building, Bismarck, 74
Lignite (coal), 16, 19, 45, 47, **56,** 57, 80, 81
Lignite (town), 57
Lincoln, Abraham, 36, 67
Lindberg, N.P., 70
Lisa, Manuel, 35
Lisbon (town), 70
Little Beaver River, 63
Little Big Horn River, Montana, 9
Little Country Theatre, Fargo, 77
Little Missouri (Medora), 63, 65

Little Missouri River, 13, **13,** 15, 63, 65, 81
Livestock, 54
Lodges, Indian, 23
Long Lake, 15
Louisiana Purchase, 30
Lounsberry, C.A., 10
Lowest point, state, 87
Maltese Cross Ranch, **95**
Mandan (city), 9, 22, 45, 67, 75
Mandan Indians, 12, 22, 23, **24,** 26-28, **27,** 29, 30, 31, 32, 74, 75
Manitoba, Canada, 11, 83
Manitoba Escarpment, 11
Mannhaven, 35
Manual training, 72
Manufacturing, 54-57
Maple River, 12
Maris, Roger, 68
Marmarth, 63
Marsh, Grant, 9, 10, 58, 70
McGregor, 57
McKenzie, Alexander, 41
McKinley, William, 65
Mayville, 71
Mdweakanton Indians, 22
Meat packing, 55, 65
Medora, 17, 20, 55, 63, 64, 65, 68, 81
Memorial Hall, Capitol, Bismarck, 74
Menoken, 29
Miller, Edgar, 74
Miller, John, 42
Miner, Hazel, 70
Minerals and mining, 45, 47, 57, 58
Minneapolis, MN, 61
Minnesota, 11, 18, 36, 60, 75, 77, 78
Minnetaree Indians, 22, **24,** 33
Minot, Henry D., 79
Minot (city), 45, 71, 79, 80
Minuteman II missiles, 78
Missiles, 78
Missions and missionaries, 46, 70, 84
Mississippi River, 16
Missouri Escarpment, 11
Missouri Fur Company, 35
Missouri Plateau, 11
Missouri River, 10, 11, 12, 13, 14, 16, 22, 26, 28, 30, 31, 33, 34, 35, 36, 40, 58, 59, 60, 74
Missouri Slope region, 11, 54
Mix, Tom, 68
Montana, 9, 11, 12, 29, 35, 36, 38
Moodie, Thomas H., 44
Moore, Henry J., 83

Moorhead, MN, 60, 75
Moraines, 18
Mores, Marquis de, 54, 65, 66, 81
Mores, Marquise de, 65, 66
Motto, state, 87
Mounds, prehistoric, 21
Mountain (town), 45
Mountains, 15
Museums, 74, 79, 81, 85
National Association of Gardeners of America, 83
National game preserve, 51, 84
National Guard, 43
National memorial park, **17, 19,** 67, 81, 95
National monument, 83
National wildlife refuge, 79
Natural gas, 19, 47, 57
Newspapers, 61
New Town, 80
New York Herald, 10
Nicknames, state, 48, 87
Nicollet, Jean, 35
Nomadic tribes, 22, 25, 28
Nonpartisan League, 43
Norse explorers, 29
North Dakota Agricultural College, 71
North Dakota Mill, 44
North Dakota plan, 72
North Dakota Rural Rehabilitation Corp., 45
North Dakota State University, Fargo, 68, 71
Northern Pacific Railroad, 42, 60, 75
North West Company, 30, 35
Northwestern Fur Company, 35
Norwegian Independence Day, 67
Norwegian people, 45, 67
Nye, Gerald P., 69
Oahe Dam, SD, 14
Oakes, 18
Oak Grove Park, Fargo, 77
Oil, 19, 45, 47, 57
Old Main, University of North Dakota, 71
Old Slant Village, 26, 74
Olson, Ole, 44
Olstad, Einar, 67
Omega All-Weather Navigation System, 45
Opals, 47
Opera house, Fargo, 77
Ordway (of Lewis and Clark party), 31
Oriental Room, Fritz Library, University of North Dakota, 78

93

Ottertail River, 12
Oxcarts, 61
Park River, 13
Parks, **17, 19,** 21, 26, 67, 74, 77, 78, 79, 80, 81, 83
Parshall, 20
Pelicans, 51
Pembina, 30, 35, 37, 46, 49, 72, 78, 85
Pembina Escarpment, 11
Pembina Mountains, 15, 46
Pembina River, 12, 18, 29
Pembina State Monument and Museum, 85
People, 45, 46, 89
Petrified wood, 19, **19,** 47
Petroglyphs, 21, 28
Petroleum, 19, 45, 47, 57
Pheasant, 51
Physiographic regions, 11
Pictographs, 21, 28
Pierce, Gilbert, 42
Pioneer Family (statue), 74, **86**
Plants, 52
Poet laureate, North Dakota, 9
Population figures, 38, 46, 87
Portal, 85
Prairie Breezes, 67
Prairie dogs, 48, **48,** 81
Prairie Fires of the Great West (Currier and Ives print), **40**
Prairie hunter (Currier and Ives print), **37**
Prehistoric times, 16, 18, 19, 21
Presbyterian church, 46, 71
Presidents, U.S., 32, 36, 42, 63, 65
Prickly pear cactus, 52
Progressive Republican Party, 43
Provencher, Joseph, 46
Pulitzer Prize, 67
Quarries, 21, 26
Rae, John A., 64
Railroads, 38, **40,** 42, 43, 60
Rain dance, Indian, 26, 27
Rainfall, 20
Ranching, 39, 40
Ranch Life and the Hunting Trail, 64
Recall vóting, 44
Red Lake River, 78
Red River of the North, 12, 14, **14,** 36, 58, 60, 75, 77, 78
Red River Valley, 11, 15, 16, 18, 29, 39, 46, 48, 53, 54, 60
Reeves, Bud, 69
Religion, 46, 70
Reno, Marcus, 9, 10
Republican Party, 43
Reservations, Indian, 46, 85

Reservoirs, 14, 15
Rhame, 83
Richland County, 67
Riverdale, 84
Rivers, 12-14
Roads, 61
Robert Campbell (steamer), 58
Rolette, Joseph, 38
Rolla, 15
Roosevelt, Theodore, 50, 63-65, 66, 67, 74, 80, 81
Roosevelt, Theodore, statue of, **62,** 80
Ross, 46
Rough Rider Hotel, Medora, 65, 81
Rough Riders, 65, 83
Round Lake, 15
Rugby (town), 70, 85
Running Antelope (Indian), 70
Rush Lake, 15
Rush River, 12
Russian thistle, 52
Rye, 54
Sacajawea, 34, 74
Saint-Memin, 32
St. Michael's Mission, 70, 84
Sandstone, 16
Saskatchewan, Canada, 11
Sauger (fish), 51
"Say it with flowers," 70
School of Mines, University of North Dakota, 57, 72
Schools, 71, 72
Scoria (clinker), 47, 58, 81
Scoria lily, 52
Scottish immigrants, 35
Sculptors, 67, 74
Sebens, William P. (Bill), 46
Selkirk, Earl of, 35
Senators, U.S., 35, 42, 69, 71
Sevareid, Eric, 68
Seventh United States Cavalry, 9, 38
Sheyenne River, 12, 14, 22
Sibley, Henry Hastings, 36
Sioux City, IA, 41
Sioux Indians, 9, 11, 12, 15, 16, 22, 31, 36, 37, 38, 39, 70, 84
Sisseton Indian reservation, 46
Sisseton Indians, 23
Sitting Bull, 38, 39, 42, 80, 85
Skyline Drive, Devils Lake, 84
Slaughter, Linda, 68
Slope, The, 11, 54
Smallpox, 29, 35
Snake Indians, 33
Sodium sulphate, 47
Soil, 18, 48, 52, 53
Song, state, 87

Souris Loop Refuges, 51
Souris River, 12, 18
South Dakota, 11, 12, 13, 14, 18, 22, 29, 36, 38, 42, 60, 61
Spain, 30
Spanish American War, 43, 64
Spring Lake Park, Williston, 80
Stagecoaches, 61
Standing Rock Indian reservation, 46, 85
Stanley, 83
Stark County, 64
State Game and Fish Commission, 52
State Historical Society, 66
State Historical Society Museum, Bismarck, 74
Statehood, 42
State Normal and Industrial School, Ellendale, 72
State parks, 21, 26, 27, 74, 78, 79, 80, 83
State School for the Blind, Grand Forks, 72
State School for the Deaf, Devils Lake, 72
State Soil Conservation Committee, 52
State Water Conservation Commission, 52
Statistics, 87
Statuary Hall, Capitol, Washington, D.C., 43
Steamboats, **8,** 9, 58, 59, **59,** 60
Stefansson, Vilhjalmur, 69
Stokes, Olive M., 68
Stone, state, 87
Strip mining, 45
Stump Lake, 15
Sublette and Campbell Company, 35
Subsistence Homestead Project, 45
Sully, Alfred H., 15, 36, 81
Sullys Hills National Game Preserve, 51, 84
Summer School of Fine Arts, International Peace Gardens, 72
Sun Dance, Indian, 28
Sunflowers, 52
Supreme Court, state, 44
Swedish people, 45
Sweet Briar Lake, 15
Symbols, state, 87
Syrian people, 46
Taft, Lorado, 67
Tappen, 36
Taylor, Joseph Henry, 68
Television tower, KTHI-TV, 77

94

Temperatures, 20
Tepee rings, 21
Tepees, 25
Teton Sioux Indians, 23
Thayer, James Bradley, 42
Theodore Roosevelt National Memorial Park, **17, 19,** 67, 81, 95
Theodore Roosevelt Park, Minot, 80
Thompson, David, 30
Tioga, 57
Titanothere, 20
Tongue Park River, 12
Tourism, 61
Townley, A.C., 43
Trading posts, 30, 35, 36
Transportation, 58-61
Tree, state, 87
Trees, 52
Turtle effigies, 21
Turtle Mountain Indian reservation, 46
Turtle Mountains, 15, 29, 52, 83
Turtle River, 12
Turtle River State Park, 78
Ukranian people, 46
United States Bureau of Mines, 57
United States Geological Survey, 85
Universities, 71, 72
University of North Dakota, Grand Forks, 57, 69, 71, 72, 78
Uranium, 45
Valley City, 71
Van Dyke brown (coloring material), 57
Varennes, Pierre Gaultier de, 29
Vérendrye, François, 29
Vérendrye, Louis-Joseph, 29
Vérendrye, Sieur de la, 29
Vérendrye National Monument, 83
Vice-Presidents, U.S., 65
Vikings, 29
Voices of Song, 67
Von Hoffman, Medora, 65
Wahpekute Indians, 23
Wahpeton (city), 12, 49, 67
Wahpeton Indians, 23
Wainwright, Robert, 70
Waldron, Lawrence R., 68
Washburn, 31, 68
Water reserves, 48
Welford, Walter, 44
Welk, Lawrence, 68
Wells-Fargo Company, 75
Wheat, 54, 55, 68, 69
White Butte, 15
White River, 20
Whitestone Battlefield State Park, 79
Whitestone Hill, Battle of, 36
Width, greatest, state, 87
Wild Rice River, 12, 14
Wild roses, 52
Wilkins, Sir Hubert, 69
Williston, 45, 71, 80
Wilton, 46
Wind Canyon, Little Missouri River, **13**
Winnipeg, Canada, 12, 61, 78
Winship, George, 78
Wisconsin glacier, 16
World War I, 43, 66, 69
World War II, 45
Writing Rock State Park, 20
Wyoming, 36, 38
XY Company, 30
Yankton, SD, 36, 41
Yanktonai Indians, 22
Yankton Indians, 22
Yellowstone (steamboat), 58
Yellowstone River, 10, 13, 34, 67
Zoos, 80

Maltese Cross Ranch, Roosevelt Headquarters, in Theodore Roosevelt National Memorial Park.

PICTURE CREDITS

Color photographs courtesy of the following: Travel Division, North Dakota State Highway Department, pages 2-3, 17 (bottom), 39, 50, 53, 62, 66, 73, 82, 86, 90 (bottom); Travelers Insurance Company, 8, 37, 40; USDI, NPS, Theodore Roosevelt National Memorial Park, 13, 17 (top), 19, 95; Fargo Chamber of Commerce, 14, 55, 76; North Dakota Park Service, 24, 27; Texas State Department of Highways and Public Transportation, 48; Department of the Army, Missouri River Division Corps of Engineers, 50, 84, 85, 90 (top); American Natural Resources Company, Detroit, MI, 56; Gilcrease Institute, 59; Jamestown Chamber of Commerce, 79.

Illustrations on back cover by Len W. Meents.

ABOUT THE AUTHOR

With the publication of his first book for school use when he was twenty, **Allan Carpenter** began a career as an author that has spanned more than 135 books. After teaching in the public schools of Des Moines, Mr. Carpenter began his career as an educational publisher at the age of twenty-one when he founded the magazine *Teachers Digest*. In the field of educational periodicals, he was responsible for many innovations. During his many years in publishing, he has perfected a highly organized approach to handling large volumes of factual material: after extensive traveling and having collected all possible materials, he systematically reviews and organizes everything. From his apartment high in Chicago's John Hancock Building, Allan recalls, "My collection and assimilation of materials on the states and countries began before the publication of my first book." Allan is the founder of Carpenter Publishing House and of Infordata International, Inc., publishers of *Issues in Education* and *Index to U. S. Government Periodicals*. When he is not writing or traveling, his principal avocation is music. He has been the principal bassist of many symphonies, and he managed the country's leading non-professional symphony for twenty-five years.